ARNOLD
WESKER

WORLD DRAMATISTS

ARNOLD WESKER

RONALD HAYMAN

With halftone illustrations

FREDERICK UNGAR PUBLISHING CO.
NEW YORK

First American publication 1973

© 1970, 1973 by Ronald Hayman
Printed in the United States of America
Library of Congress Catalog Card Number: 78-153120
Designed by Edith Fowler
ISBN 0-8044-2387-3 (cloth)

ACKNOWLEDGMENTS

The author and publisher wish to thank Arnold Wesker and Jonathan Cape for permission to reprint extracts from *Roots, The Four Seasons, I'm Talking about Jerusalem, Chips with Everything, Their Very Own and Golden City, The Kitchen, Chicken Soup with Barley, The Friends, The Old Ones*, and *The Journalists*.

The photographs from *Roots, The Kitchen* and *Their Very Own and Golden City* are reproduced by courtesy of the Royal Court Theatre.

CONTENTS

CHRONOLOGY

1932   Born in Stepney. His father was a Russian tailor, his mother a Hungarian. She often had to support the family by working in kitchens.

1943   At Upton House School, Hackney, where besides the normal curriculum he was trained in book-keeping, typing and shorthand.

1948   Started a variety of jobs—apprentice to a furniture maker, mate to a carpenter, and assistant in a bookshop.

1950–2   National Service in R.A.F.

1951   Started work on a novel, *The Reed that Bent*, in April. Finished it in August.

1952–8   Another series of jobs: assistant in another bookshop, plumber's mate, seed sorter, farm laborer, builder's laborer, kitchen porter, trainee pastrycook. As a pastrycook in Paris, he saved up enough money to pay for a course at the London School of Film Technique.

1953   Started *And After Today*, a play, parts of which are incorporated into *Chicken Soup with Barley*.

1955   Began a short play, "Pools," in October.

1956   Wrote *The Kitchen*.

1957   Started *Chicken Soup with Barley* (originally titled *When the Wind Blows*) in October.

1958   Arts Council award of £300. Started *Roots* in June, finished second typed draft in October. Married Doreen Cecile Bicker in November. Started work on *I'm Talking about Jerusalem* in December.

1959   Won *Evening Standard* award as Most Promising Dramatist of the Year.

1960   Started work on *Chips with Everything* in September, and finished the first typed draft in December.

1961   Film version of *The Kitchen* released in the United States. Started work on a television play, *Menace*, in May, finishing the first typed draft in September. Served a month in prison for activities in protest against nuclear weapons. Appointed director of Centre 42, a movement he launched to secure trade union backing for the arts.

1962   Wrote the libretto for Wilfred Josephs' opera *The Nottingham Captain* in June for the Wellingborough Festival.

1963   Began work on *Their Very Own and Golden City* in January and finished the first typed draft in November. The original title *Congress* was dropped when the Kama Sutra came out in a popular edition.

1964   Started *The Four Seasons* in May.

1965   Finished *The Four Seasons* in September. Finished working on *Their Very Own and Golden City* which had now been through nine drafts.

1966   Wrote a short story, "Six Sundays in January." Started work on *The Friends* in July.

1968   Finished second draft of *The Friends* in July.

1969   Started work on *The Old Ones*.

1970   Persuaded the council of Centre 42 to dissolve itself.

1971   Spent eight weeks in the office of *The Sunday Times* and afterward wrote the book *Journey into Journalism*.

1972   Completed the fifth draft of *The Old Ones* in February and the fifth draft of a new play, *The Journalists*, in April.

FIRST INTERVIEW

RONALD HAYMAN: *You said in a lecture last year, "I'd like people to know me not only by my writing but by my life."*

ARNOLD WESKER: At a time when there is so much fraudulence and personality-cultifying and a general air of dishonesty, even in the areas supposed to be free and liberated, brave and honest—by which I mean the pop areas and the hip scene—I find in myself a compulsion to try as much as possible not to cheat and to let people know about me personally. I don't really succeed and I know I could never succeed, because there are areas of me which I'm desperately ashamed of or unhappy about and would hate to be revealed to anyone. Also, the need for honesty shouldn't ever step over the bounds of taste . . . I suspect one of my motives for wanting to be as honest as possible is also to disarm as much criticism as possible. I think that with all artists the act of exposing themselves is really the act of treating themselves as a guinea pig, saying, "Look, this is what I've been through. This is how I have seen it or feel about it or suffered about it or been happy about it, and I think you ought to know just in case you can beware of it or share it. But I have both been through it and also dared to go through it."

3

You've divided your time between writing and organizing Centre 42. If you could redraft your life as you can a play, what alterations would you make?

That's a luscious prospect. I would make myself more ruthless and try to be the one person who could manage to be ruthless without having it damage his personality so that one was ruthless for the Good and the Romantic, and in that way make more of a success of Centre 42 while at the same time not damaging myself as a writer.

You don't believe that Centre 42 would have taken up so much working time that you wouldn't have been able to write?

No. I really think that when it's upon you, when you really *must*, you find it, you work to all hours of the morning. I mean you make time, you just do it. You can snatch half hours between interviews, even at the office. I virtually wrote *The Kitchen* in between serving sweets at the Hungaria Restaurant. I thought about it at least and made notes. But now, because I've got the dead weight of a feeling of failure to lift up before I can write I need to go away to Wales. It's almost impossible to work here in London.

Ronald Bryden wrote in the introduction to one of your plays that it's less important that you should become a complete artist than remain a unique outsider in our theater.

I think in the end I would sooner be a complete artist. Anyway, there are so few complete artists that to ever achieve this would make one a unique outsider.

You once said yourself, "I am not sure that really great art leads one immediately to action, and I think possibly this is why my plays aren't great art."

I really don't think that any artistic manifestation leads immediately to action, whether it's great art or not. What I meant vis-à-vis my plays is that one comes away with a more immediate feeling about them. I don't think they grow on you, I don't think this is the kind of thing that has a delayed action, with the possible exception of *The Four Seasons*. All the others are fairly simple immediate theatrical pieces.

How do your parents compare with Harry and Sarah Kahn in the trilogy?

Almost totally. They are—in so far as it is possible—total re-creations. So are most of the characters, with the only exception of me. The character of me I take liberties with. I put myself in the weak role in order that alongside Ronnie, Sarah Kahn can emerge, and alongside Ronnie in *Jerusalem*, Dave and Ada can emerge. And in *Roots*, Beatie can emerge. *Roots* was written after Dusty and I were married, so the fabrication of them not marrying could be seen as an attack on me, but it doesn't bear with the truth. I was just using myself.

What was your childhood like?

Well, my memory of it is smashing, and I'm always dreaming about the East End. It wasn't for my sister—she always remembers it with horror. But I was a ruffian—I think generally known as a charming ruffian—but tended to overstep the mark and would earn slaps from people who had never slapped before in their lives. For instance, an uncle—a marvelously sweet, gentle uncle—was moved to crack me round the face one day when I was tantalizing his daughter, my cousin. And another uncle whom I just persistently irritated by plucking his braces while he was eating his dinner of chips and egg. And a French schoolmaster whom I loved—I was the only boy he ever caned.

There's something about me which attracts finally this hostility. It's been recurrent through my life. As a child I used to play truant, and I used to find myself the leader of gangs, the one who always dared most. Do you remember those water tanks [used as reservoirs] during the air raids? There were always stories of kids getting drowned in them. With some friends I made a balsa-wood raft, and we all decided we would float on it in this tank. And when it came to it, I was the only one that did and was caught by a policeman who took me off and was taking me home to report me to my parents. On the journey from that tank to my door, at the last minute I succeeded in persuading him not to.

Those are the extremes. And then you get repetitions of it in later life. I am able to persuade Louis Mintz* to give me the Roundhouse but rouse the hostility of a man like Robert Maxwell,† or even Jennie Lee [the Labour Government's Minister for the Arts] in the end. I think because there is a level at which I really mean what I say about a lot of things, and I'm the one person who looks as though he really is capable of going over the border and doing it. At the height of 42 I really was capable of selling up almost everything and raising money for 42. I would go to extremes. And I think people like Jennie recognized that I was capable of biting the hand that fed me. I'm only just realizing this as I'm saying it, but there is, I think, a consistent pattern which was like this in childhood and can be seen now.

I enjoyed the East End. It didn't worry me that we were poor. I enjoyed the street life. There were aunts and a grandmother next door. There were times when I was distressed by the rows between my parents, but there was a life in the household, a political and social life, and they were also parents whom I adored individually so it somehow didn't

* Chairman of the House of Selincourt, a group of companies dealing in textiles, etc., which at Wesker's urging gave Centre 42 the Roundhouse, a disused shed, for use as a theater.

† MP and chairman of Pergamon Press, he became Honorary Treasurer of Centre 42.

matter. I was obviously able to survive the rows. Although it's left its mark in that you can probably trace through all the plays the theme of the male-female relationship. It's obviously there between Sarah and Harry in *Chicken Soup*. It takes on a different form in *Roots*. In *Jerusalem* it's not only there between Ada and Dave but Libby Dobson, the cynic, when he comes. It takes on a special shape in *Menace*, the television play. There is the embryo of *The Four Seasons*. In *The Four Seasons* it is the pure male-female battle. It's also there in *Golden City*. So to this extent I'm conscious that their battles must have made an impression. I don't know—I may be preoccupied with the sex war because of my own experiences.

One of the things that I've inherited from my parents is a kind of intense fear of brutishness—of the *Lumpenproletariat*. That's why characters like the boys in Edward Bond's *Saved* affect me in a very particular way. I curl up at them and—yes, this has only just occurred to me—this is what links the plays to Centre 42 and this is why I have always thought of *Roots* as a Jewish play. It's a fear, inherited from the community, of that brutish quality and the feeling that something needs to be done against it. Because it's dangerous.

What sort of religious life was there in your home?

None. There was a moment when I thought I suddenly wanted to go to Yeshiva [religious training school], and I think I stuck that out for four weeks. I wasn't bar mitzvahed. I just had a thirteenth birthday party—a large one, paid for by the one rich uncle in the family, who also bought me a wrist watch which was promptly stolen in the swimming baths.

So this consciousness of Jewishness has nothing to do with the Jewish religion?

No.

Has it to do with community life in Jewish terms at all?

The Jewishness I took for granted. I only began to think specially about Jewishness when I was about fourteen, when I joined *Habonim* [a Jewish youth group]. My Jewish consciousness was deepened and sharpened during that period, which was about four or five years. And then it lapsed entirely and it's only recently—in the last possibly three years—that I felt Jewish in a *belonging* way or a protective way. I think that what happens is that you are suddenly aware that you have inherited a shared consciousness of your community's suffering. I didn't experience much anti-Semitism as a child. What I did discover I took fairly flippantly. I mean I had socialist answers for why it existed. And we were a long way from what happened in Europe to the other Jews. But there does remain an inherited sense of a history of persecution. And it is that which I think gives one a sense of identity.

Was the novel about the Air Force the first thing that you wrote?

No it wasn't. The first thing that I wrote was a poem called "The Breeze," at the age of twelve. I wrote hundreds of poems and many short stories and then the novel. That was the first major attempt.

This mixture of jobs you did, what was the sequence?

On leaving school, I was apprenticed to a furniture maker who was making antique reproductions. I became redundant because he was working on his own and the competition became too great and he couldn't afford to keep me. I left him to become a carpenter's mate for a building firm with whom I stayed something like ten months, a year perhaps. Left that to work in a bookshop, Simmonds of Fleet Street, where I stayed for possibly eighteen months. Left that for a short period working for Robert Copping* in his basement bookshop. That didn't last for long. I went shortly afterwards into the Air Force for two years short of two months. Came out and worked in another bookshop, Stonehams of Old Broad Street.

This was when you tried to get into the Royal Academy of Dramatic Art?

Yes. Then worked as a plumber's mate on the docks for about six months. Then moved to Norfolk, lived with my sister and had this vast assortment of jobs—as a seed sorter and as a farm laborer and as a builder's laborer.

Was it because of your sister that you went to Norfolk, or because of this girl friend who wanted to marry a farmer?

There were three things. I wanted to get away from London. Norfolk was a good place to get away to because my sister and brother-in-law were there and I was so fond of them. And Olive [my girl friend] also wanted to leave London and be in the country because she had a hankering for country life. It was during the period that we were living with my sister that she let it be known that she really wanted to marry a farmer, and so we went to these dances and we used to pretend we were brother and sister. We actually looked like each other in a strange way. This was my way of helping her to find a farmer and that was exactly what happened. At the local country hop one farmer, Charlie English, dated her and there was this ridiculous situation.

* Originally headmaster of England's first progressive school, Horsley Hall, Staffordshire. After the school was closed, at one point Copping ran a bookshop on Kensington Church Street.

Now you see there's a consistency—I put myself in a position where she could get what she wanted, because this was what I could offer her, just like in the plays I put myself in a position so that some of the other characters can emerge. And she got married. I became very distressed, and then I went to Norwich and there worked as a kitchen porter for about eighteen months and then came to London and met Dusty there. Dusty fell in love with me there and I told her she was a fool and that she could expect nothing from me.

I'd been turned down by all my girl friends actually. Every girl that I'd ever fallen for had rejected me and so I'd come to the conclusion there was something wrong with me, and would never ever be able to fall in love or have anyone fall in love with me. In order to dissuade Dusty from finding me attractive—I used to have a mop of marvelous hair—I went to the barber's and got a crew cut down to about half an inch because I thought this would make me ugly. She was very annoyed, but it didn't put her off.

Anyway then I left and worked in the Hungaria Restaurant in Lower Regent Street. And that's where I was a trainee pastrycook. I left Dusty on the understanding that there shouldn't be anything more between us, but she said she wanted to go to London anyway and look for work and I said, "If I can be of any help I will be." She came to London and worked as a waitress, and our relationship continued. Then I wanted to get away from London again, and I decided that the restaurant was to be my career. I wanted to extend my experience and decided to go to Paris. Dusty came with me to Paris as an *au pair* and I worked in this restaurant Le Rallye for six months. Then read an advert about a film school. I'd always missed not being a student and was able to save up enough money in this Paris restaurant to pay for a six-month course at the London School of Film Technique. And so we came back and I studied at the London School, which was useless, really.

But you'd given up the idea of writing?

I'd decided that I wanted to write and direct films.

But in that black period after your girl friend married the farmer, you didn't want to be an actor or a writer?

No, I'd decided quite happily to settle down and be a kitchen porter. And it was a very splendid feeling—the only time in my life free from any kind of ambition and I really enjoyed the whole period. It was a sort of cleansing period. And out of it came the first work. Because I used to cheat and make notes and pretend that I wasn't really writing, somehow. The first work that I felt really had any merit was a trilogy of stories. And while I was at the London School of Film Technique I asked Lindsay Anderson* whether he would read *The Kitchen*, and I sent it to the *Observer* Play Competition. And when it was turned down by the *Observer* I didn't bother him with it. But I asked him to read "Pools" [a short story]—I thought it would make a good film for the Experimental Film Fund. And he read it and liked it and passed it on to Karel Reisz,* who read it and liked it, and put it up to the committee. But they all decided I hadn't had enough experience to make it. And then I wrote *Chicken Soup* and I felt so good about this that I was prepared to risk bothering him with it to read.

When did you start writing full time?

I can remember earning some small amounts of money from *Chicken Soup*. Then I can remember getting an advance of £25 for *Roots*, which the [Royal] Court [Theatre] turned down. I got the Arts Council grant of £250, which I spent on our wedding. How was I living then? I think I must have

---

* Anderson and Reisz are film directors.

been living off Dusty, who was working at Sainsbury's [a grocery chain], earning £7 10s. to £8.

Where were you living then?

I was living at home at Clapton Common, with my parents, in a flat. Then when we got married we moved to a basement flat not far from my mother, and then afterwards we moved to Gloucester Drive, in Finsbury Park, to a ground–floor flat, and in 1962 moved here [Highgate]. So that would also indicate the rate at which royalties began coming in.

When did your involvement in 42 start?

It began with this lecture that I gave at Oxford when the *Sunday Times* had the Student Drama Festival there and they asked me to come up and talk about the contemporary playwright. I gave a lecture which was an attack on the Labour movement for neglecting the role of art and the artist in society. And then I turned that lecture into a pamphlet and sent it to every General Secretary in the country and then followed that up with a second pamphlet making suggestions. One of the suggestions was that the T.U.C. [Trades Union Congress] should hold an inquiry into the state of the arts and this was the suggestion that the A.C.T.T. [Association of Cinematograph Television and Allied Technicians] took up and made a resolution at that year's T.U.C. Congress, which was number 42 on the agenda.

At the same time, Doris Lessing was talking to me about a group of writers and television directors and others who were getting together because they were generally dissatisfied with the role they were playing. They wanted to make contact with a larger and more popular audience. One of the things I was determined not to do was to become involved with another well-meaning left-wing little cultural enterprise. I managed to insist on a larger and more serious view of what should be done and generally outlined the idea which finally became

Centre 42, but which was added to by various members of that committee. We were going to be the initiators of such a center, the council, the board. At no time had I intended to take on the running of it, but no one emerged from outside who looked as though they either could or would take on such a big and uncertain thing.

I think it was while I was serving a term in prison for my activities with the Committee of 100[*] that I thought about it and decided that I must make a total commitment. So I put myself forward to be the artistic director of it, and it was generally agreed. But bit by bit most of the others dropped away because it all became too ambitious for them. I saw Centre 42 not only as an attempt to create something that would reach a wider audience, but as a project that would consolidate and give a continuing outlet to that whole band of new writers and directors and actors, whom I instinctively felt would be dismissed in a very short time because of the fashion-conscious rhythms of the cultural world. There was a period when they suddenly got tired of what became known as the Kitchen Sink writers, and it seemed to me that someone like Shelagh Delaney particularly suffered from this fashion-conscious approach.

What was the relationship between Chips *and the novel?*

Very simply the different scenes approximated to the chapters in the novel. Certainly the characters are drawn from characters in the novel, who are drawn from characters in the Air Force. I'd decided that I was going to write something about square-bashing [drilling recruits], and so every day I wrote home a long letter to a friend or relative and asked them to keep it. Then I assembled them all at the end in chronological order, and from those letters created the novel. That's how it was done.

In thinking about the structure of my work I have come to

[*] Group of celebrities protesting nuclear armament.

consider a possible theory about the composition of any work of art. On the assumption that all art is the re-creation of experience whether imaginative or actual, then the re-creative act happens under two headings, both of which are valid. One heading could be called "the organization of experience" and the other "the transformation of experience"—transformation, that is, into poetry. And from such a theory one should then analyze a work of art to discover how much is organizing and how much is transforming an experience. The more moments of transformation one can find, the greater the work of art. This doesn't invalidate the need for the organizing process. Seventy-five percent of *Roots* is organization of experience. Moments such as when Beatie looks at herself in the mirror after her bath and discovers the lumps in her body—that for me is transformation into poetry. Chekhov is seventy-five percent transformation.

How did you feel about the production of Golden City?

The production really didn't work. I think Bill [Gaskill, the director,] was unhappy finally—there was a point at which he said, "I realize this just isn't my kind of play," and it needed an energy really in the production that should have been able to cover up all the structural weaknesses. It's the kind of play that should really be off the ground most of the time and never was.

I still don't really know how this device of the flash-forward could work.

I don't know either. What they did at the Court was to use just the one actor to do both the old and the young Andy Cobham. Whereas I think that seeing the old and the young immediately, one after the other—instead of devising ways of the old one disappearing and changing back to the young one—would have had an extraordinary effect. You also lost in the production what I attempted to do. I attempted to have a parallel action between the youthful enthusiasm of 1928 as a present, a moment of now, alongside which one could measure the way in which experience forces one to deviate, in the future, from all these hopes and dreams. I wanted one to be constantly confronted with such a measurement. The flash-forward would have been a way of giving people an opportunity to measure what they are now with what they remember of their past in a way that the normal technique of flashback wouldn't . . . I think there's something more urgent about developing a future than tracing back a past in order to make a point.

Yes, but if you show a flash-forward, you're implying that there's a possibility that it could develop differently from that—there's not quite the same sort of fatalism about it.

Yes. I got away with two endings. I satisfied that part of me which is constantly in conflict, that part of me which wants to encourage an energy based on hope tempered by the knowledge of the pessimistic possibilities. And the way in which I had done it with the other plays . . . for instance in *Chicken Soup* I start at the top and go all the way down, I mean to rock bottom, as far down as I can go and then have Sarah give her speech. I don't think it's a false adding on at the end because what she's saying is very consistent with what she is throughout the play, but it also serves my purpose of taking things down to the lowest possible depths of depression and failure before coming up. And the same with *Roots*, and the same with *Jerusalem*. But *Golden City* does it in a different way. It just has the two running side by side.

Golden City obviously derives from Centre 42.

Yes.

To what extent are you disillusioned?

In *The Friends* Macey says that one of the disciplines he had to learn was not to elevate his own personal disappointments to the level of a universal philosophy—not to equate his failures with all men's failures. I think there are such extraordinary things that happen that it's an impertinence to talk about being disillusioned with life and the world. If one has failed oneself that's something else, and if one's experience is to have touched only other failures, that's also something else. But to presume that such experience can indicate global awfulness about life and . . . I will go on record with a hundred percent prophecy that things like Centre 42 will be existing all over the country sooner or later. All that's happened is that I've failed to bring it about.

But this isn't a personal failure.

Oh, I think so.

Surely it isn't a question of one person's ability. With Centre 42 the whole question of the relationship with the Trade Union movement, the Labour Party and the arts is absolutely of the essence. You expected the Trades Unions to become involved in a way in which they weren't prepared to. This is not your failure.

Surely if I'd been a different kind of person I might have known the right way to systematically go through not only those general secretaries but the whole of my social life would have been dedicated to mixing in Trade Union circles and slowly, slowly building up personal relationships with all the right people. I obviously didn't have that quality that knew how to use to the best advantage all the people whose attachments I could command as a playwright. That's what I'm led to conclude.

But perhaps what you wanted just wasn't attainable.

Yes, it perhaps wasn't attainable. But it was possible. I mean 42 was possible because there was the artistic energy on the one hand and there was a feeling in all sorts of areas of the rank and file that 42 was at last something they'd all been waiting for because it measured up to their concept of the good, the marvelous life that socialism had always been about. So there were those two feelings. What there wasn't was the kind of courage at leadership level—that's what made it unattainable. But given the money it could all have worked.

What about the transition from Golden City *to* The Four Seasons?

You could say that *The Four Seasons* was the story of Kate and Andrew Cobham taking a year's sabbatical off from building the Golden City and spending it in a deserted house.

PLAYS

The Kitchen

The merits and faults of any dramatist's work must to some extent reflect those of his personality and the more autobiographical his plays are the clearer the reflection is likely to be. But no one—not even Strindberg—has resembled his own plays as closely as Wesker resembles his. They are warm, humane, sincere, passionate, compassionate, brave, honest, energetic, outspoken, full of enthusiasm, full of concern. The enthusiasm is largely enthusiasm for the possibilities of enjoying life and enjoying art as an integral part of it. The concern is partly concern about social pressures that prevent the vast bulk of society from coming alive sufficiently to enjoy either life or art as much as it could.

Wesker's main faults as a playwright are the faults that would naturally accompany these virtues. He is didactic. He tends to let the social problem distract him from his characters' personal predicaments. He is prone to wordiness, ingenuousness and over-emotionality. He is too passionate about what he is saying to be careful about how he says it. He depends less on his intellect than on his instinct, which sometimes leads him to brilliant formal inventions, but he is neither self-critical nor very conscious of technical problems. Consequently, there is a hit-or-miss quality about his writing, and his construction, though sometimes excellent, is often weaker than it would be if he were more aware of working in a tradition, more interested in how other playwrights have solved—or failed to solve—technical problems. But it is also true that if he were technically more self-conscious, he might be less uninhibited.

He has taken risks which others would have thought fool-hardy, but he has succeeded in bringing a kind of life to the English stage that was never there before. There had been plenty of working-class characters in plays written before *Look Back in Anger* (1956), but no one had ever cut such large slices of the working life of the working classes and bundled them so unceremoniously on to a stage, saying, in effect, "See how little I have to transcribe in order to give you drama." In 1955 no one would have thought it possible to make a large-scale success out of a play with twenty-nine characters and with the whole action set in a kitchen. No one would have thought that a trilogy of plays about Jewish communists and Norfolk farm laborers would stand the remotest chance of being produced. And no one could have guessed that the West End would welcome an all-male play about National Service which grows into a swinging attack on our whole social system and ends with the National Anthem played to a seated audience.

It was hard, at first, for Wesker to get his plays accepted, even at the fairly avant-garde Royal Court. Rather than risk their own production of *Chicken Soup with Barley*, George Devine, the Artistic Director, and Tony Richardson, his associate, took advantage of a grant that the Arts Council was offering to repertory theaters that produced new plays. They sent the script to the Belgrade Theater, Coventry, and then staged the Coventry production for one week, together with three other new plays from three other repertory theaters, each played for a week. When Wesker then offered them *Roots*, George Devine and Tony Richardson tried to persuade him to write a scene in which Ronnie appeared. Even after *Roots* (which also opened in Coventry and transferred) was such a great success, they were so convinced that *The Kitchen* could not be made to work theatrically that John Dexter, who had directed *Chicken Soup with Barley* and *Roots*, had great difficulty in persuading them to let him try it out even for a Sunday night production.

Wesker's plays have always been treated to extreme reactions. After the initial bout of rebuffs and rejections, they were greeted by the critics with words like "great" and "masterpiece." His reputation in England was at its height between 1959, when *Roots* made such a huge impact, and 1962, when *Chips with Everything* transferred triumphantly to the West End. He has enjoyed many successes abroad since 1962, but in London critics have rebounded from overestimating his achievement into underestimating it. *Their Very Own and Golden City* failed to transfer from the Royal Court to the West End and *The Four Seasons,* his first play not to be staged at the Court, started in Coventry and transferred to the West End, where the critics savaged it. Some, like John Russell Taylor, in *Anger and After,* have now expressed the opinion that his early work made the impact it did "for quite other than strictly dramatic reasons." Was it just a case of a clear, young, persuasive working-class voice making itself heard at the right moment when that Trojan Horse of a Royal Court burst open inside London's middle-class theatrical stronghold? How do *The Kitchen, Chicken Soup with Barley, Chips with Everything* and Wesker's other plays stand up now that the vogue for "Kitchen Sink" drama has passed? It is time to form a balanced assessment, looking at the plays strictly as plays.

The chief source of unevenness in them is the separation that sometimes occurs between action and argument. The best moments of all in his plays are moments when a galvanic action on stage is pointedly relevant to the statement that the play is making—as it is in the organized pandemonium at the end of Act One of *The Kitchen*, when orders are being shouted, and waitresses are scurrying around the serving areas while the cooks work to dish up the food and kitchen porters —busboys—hurry to clear away dirty dishes. There is a theatrical excitement in the large-scale movement similar to that of the coke-stealing sequence in *Chips with Everything*, in which, under cover of darkness, the recruits are outwitting the guards. One of them uses a chair to clamber over the wire fence, and another removes it before the guard returns on his sentry-go. Precision of timing here is made theatrical as organized chaos was in *The Kitchen*. The end of Act Two of *Roots*, though it involves only two characters, can produce an almost comparable excitement. Here, more directly than in the other two cases, we get a taste of Wesker's own *joie de vivre* in the enthusiasm of his characters.

He is nearly always warmly sympathetic towards his characters, but he is often more interested in what they are saying than in why they are saying it. They are saying it in fact because he wants it to be said. In *Chicken Soup with Barley*, *I'm Talking about Jerusalem*, *Their Very Own and Golden City* and *The Four Seasons*, we sometimes become aware that he is using his characters and their situation to make points that were preoccupying him long before they were.

The Kitchen is less open to this criticism. It is still one of his best plays. There may be weak passages in the central section, where the characters are resting, and in the speeches at the end, but the play as a whole succeeds brilliantly in crystallizing what it has to say into its theatrical form. Above all, the image of the kitchen comes richly alive. The work of the harassed cooks and hurrying waitresses grows into a theatrical metaphor that stands for all work. The low sound of gas in the ovens, the sheer physical pressure of the labor involved in preparing meals for such a big and busy restaurant, the extra strain created by tensions between the national and racial groups, the babel of different languages, the hierarchy of the kitchen with the owner at the top, the cooks able to lord it over the waitresses and the kitchen porters at the very bottom, except for the tramp who wanders in to beg for food—all this builds up into a complex image of man as a working animal.

As Kenneth Tynan said in his review of the play, the dramatization of work is something that few playwrights have ever attempted. Most of them situate their action in the spaces between work, but Wesker (like Arthur Miller in *A Memory of Two Mondays*) shows how the rhythm of a working routine determines not only the rhythm of the relationships that are possible inside it but the rhythm of whole lives of the characters who depend on it. It is not just that everything else they do has to be fitted around their work—they are what they are because of their work, and they express themselves most directly in the way they work.

In John Dexter's productions of the play at the Royal Court—his successive productions varied slightly from each other—no food was used. The actions of the cooks were mimed but the miming was realistically worked out and the absence of actual food heightened our awareness of the movements. They characterized themselves all the more clearly through the way they dished out nonexistent fish or rolled out imaginary pastry.

The dialogue is written with a sureness of touch which is uncanny in a first play by a writer who at this time had very little playgoing experience. He handles his large cast with great skill, finding exactly the right moments to give a great many of them foreground treatment. There is a balance between the two long working sequences which are divided by an interlude set at a time when the kitchen is quiet and the cooks resting or off-duty.* The build-ups to the climaxes are

---

* I have since been told by Wesker that the interlude was written in at the suggestion of the director, John Dexter, who said it was essential to divide the two working sequences with something that would contrast with them.

all well planned and there is great expertise in the modulation between themes. Passages of reflective conversation are interspersed with incidents and accidents. Gossip about last night's fight in which one of the Cypriots nearly knifed Peter, the German fish-cook, a relaxed moment of dancing to a record player that one of the kitchen porters has made, the panic of pretending to be absorbed in work when the boss arrives, the bickering about foreigners working in England, the resentments against the boss, the chef, and the second chef, the quarrels about dates with the waitresses, a scream from the steam room where a cook knocks over a pot of hot water and burns his face—the way Wesker organizes these elements makes us believe in him totally as a chronicler of group life in the busy inferno beside the plushy paradise of an expensive restaurant.*

In many of Wesker's later plays, the framework of values is constructed over a contrast between an ideal and a necessary departure from that ideal. In *Chicken Soup with Barley, I'm Talking about Jerusalem, Their Very Own and Golden City* and *The Four Seasons,* the ideal is indicated at the beginning of the play, and the development is concerned largely with the departure. In *The Kitchen*—and in this respect it is superior —there is no such clear glimpse of an ideal and no such definite pattern of a departure from it. We get all the indications we need of a scale of values from the references to good work and bad work. The satisfaction of making a record player with one's hands is contrasted with the joylessness of working in a factory and having to devote the whole day to one component piece, making a wire or screwing on a knob. The possibility of good cooking is contrasted with the mass-

* Understandably, the designer of one of the continental productions of the play preferred to indicate that the kitchen was underneath the restaurant, not at the side of it, as it was at Le Rallye, the Paris restaurant where Wesker worked and on which he mainly based the play. It was partly based on his experience at the Hungaria.

production cooking in which only speed and quantity count. The results of working too long under these conditions are seen in the Chef, who has grown apathetic, and in three of the cooks, who are invariably drunk by the end of the day.

The first section of the play is the most nearly flawless. The opening is slow and effective. A kitchen porter lights the ovens which will go on burning audibly all through the play. The ensuing conversation may be slightly too obviously an exposition of last night's events—the quarrel and the fight—and a build-up about the relationship between Peter and Monique, a waitress. But the dance and the xenophobic bickering move the play onto firmer ground. The arrival of a new cook both facilitates a certain amount of explanation about the routine and emphasizes the length of time that some of them have been working in the same place. The racial and national prejudices and the tensions they produce profit by being shown in the context of work that involves cooperation and harmony. Wesker shows himself adept at exploiting the small-scale theatrical effectiveness of a practical joke like the one Peter plays on Frank by balancing a glass of water on top of his hat.

There is no space for Wesker to go into depth or detail about Peter's relationship with Monique, but his impatience about the break she has promised to make with her husband dovetails neatly into his unwillingness to go on working much longer in the restaurant. The pressure he is under shows in his effectively abrupt changes of mood.

> PETER: I'm not going to wait much longer, you'll see. You think I like this Tivoli? You don't believe me I won't wait do you?
> MONTIQUE: Please yourself.
> PETER (*despairingly*): What do you want me to do? Do you want to make me something to laugh at? Three years I'm here now, three . . . (*Monique leaves him, saying* "Not now."

Peter is about to become furious but controls him-
self and as though in high spirits kicks a cardboard
margarine box that has been lying around.)

PETER (*shouting*): *Auf geht's,* Irishman. Finish now.
Auf geht's.

(Peter sings his song and Hans and Kevin join in
with him as they—and indeed all the cooks—clear
away their plates and prepare to face the service.)

From this point the action builds up quickly to the highly theatrical furor of the lunch service. Faster and faster the waitresses bustle in to shout their orders at the different stations, collecting plates, clamoring, arguing, passing on, while the sweating cooks serve and shout back, and the kitchen porters clear away empty pots. The rush is at its climax when the lights fade.

Wesker has succeeded so well in his first act that he could easily have afforded to cut Dmitri's overexplicit speech from the interlude:

This stinking kitchen is like the world—you know what I mean? It's too fast to know what happens. People come and people go, big excitement, big noise. (*Makes noise, gesticulates and runs wildly about and then stops.*) What for? In the end who do you know? You make a friend, you going to be all your life his friend, but when you go from here—pshtt! you forget!

Altogether his touch is less sure here. Certainly there is value in the contrast of tempo, but it is hard to agree with the point he makes in showing that the German and the Jew get on better when there is no rush of work to be done. (Normally, cooperation in any kind of work is more likely to reduce latent hostility than to heighten it.) And the scene in which Peter invites the others to speak out their dreams is the first example in Wesker's work of a game. He makes his characters play games in every play he has written except

Chips with Everything and (for me at least) the games never work in the way they are intended to. Often the intention, as here, is simply to make the fact of speaking out into a dramatic issue. Certainly the characters reveal something about themselves by speaking out their dreams and the pastrycook tells a funny but horrifying story about a bus driver who wants a bomb dropped on the peace marchers just because the march holds up the buses. But this narrative works on a different level from everything else, and the only dramatic touch comes when Peter walks off with Monique without contributing to the game that he invented.

Act Two almost lifts the play back on to the level it reached in Act One, but not quite; it fails to achieve the same balance between foreground and background. The climax Wesker is building up to now is the moment when Peter goes berserk. The act starts off well enough with the incident of the tramp. Peter takes the watery soup the chef has given him out of his hand and gives him two cutlets. The boss, Marango, comes in while the chef is telling Peter off. In the next scene he has with Monique, Peter finds she has no serious intention of leaving her husband now that he has promised they will soon have a home of their own. Though this contributes usefully to explaining why Peter gets so desperate, it does not relate it closely enough to the main theme of the play. The quarrel Peter now has with a waitress triggers off his breakdown. She helps herself to fish without waiting for him to serve her.

> PETER: You don't worry who I am. I'm a cook, yes? And you're the waitress, and in the kitchen you do what I like, yes? And in the dining-room you do what you like.
>
> WAITRESS (*taking another plate from the oven*): I won't take orders from you, you know, I . . .
>
> PETER (*shouting and smashing the plate from her hand for a second time*): Leave it! Leave it there! I'll serve you. Me! Me! Is *my* kingdom here. This is the side where I live. *This.*
>
> WAITRESS: You Bosch you. You bloody German bastard!

She walks off and he screams at her to say it again. Frustrated in his craving for violence, he seizes a chopper, smashes it into the gas pipe, rushes into the dining room, sweeps a pile of plates off a table and rips his hands. Good though it is that the climax has interrupted the whole routine of the restaurant, the whole rhythm of Marango's world, his final speech is far too explicit:

> MARANGO: Why does everybody sabotage me, Frank? I give work, I pay well, yes? They eat what they want, don't they? I don't know what more to give a man. He works, he eats, I give him money. This is life, isn't it? I haven't made a mistake, have I? I live in the right world, don't I? (*To Peter*). And you've stoppped this world. A shnip! A boy! You've stopped it. Well why? Maybe you can tell me something I don't know—just tell me. (*No answer.*) I want to learn something. (*To Frank.*) Is there something I don't know? (*Peter rises and in pain moves off. When he reaches a point back centre stage Marango cries at him.*) BLOODY FOOL! (*Rushes round to him.*) What more do you want? What is there more, tell me? (*He shakes Peter but gets no reply. Peter again tries to leave. Again Marango cries out.*) What is there more? (*Peter stops, turns in pain and sadness, shakes his head as if to say—if you don't know I cannot explain. And so he moves right off stage. Marango is left facing his staff who stand around, almost accusingly, looking at him. And he asks again—*) What is there more? What *is* there more?

The question "What more do you want?" is apt enough, but "What is there more?" generalizes the implication in a way that distracts us uncomfortably from Marango's feelings to Wesker's intentions.

Chicken Soup with Barley

Chicken Soup with Barley, which together with *Roots* and *I'm Talking about Jerusalem* forms a trilogy, is one of the first serious and successful political plays to be written in England. As Kenneth Tynan pointed out in his review: "Nobody else has ever attempted to put a real, live, English communist family on to the stage; and the important thing about Mr. Wesker's attempt is that they *are* real, and they *do* live."

It is just as hard to fuse personal and political themes in the theater as it is in the novel, and it is just as easy to fall into the trap of writing about individuals who, because they represent a group or a political viewpoint, fail to speak with their own voices or to come to life or to develop. Wesker's instinct has worked admirably in leading him to concern himself with the changing orientation of his characters towards communism over a twenty-year period. Act One is set in 1936; Act Two starts in 1946; Act Three ends in 1956.

In 1936 it is easy for the Kahn family and their friends to see what there is to fight for and against. The Spanish Civil War is on and Dave, who is later to marry Ada Kahn, is about to go out and fight in it. Meanwhile there is trouble from the fascists nearer home. The Mosleyites are planning a demonstration in the East End, and together with other working-class groups, who have shown a splendid solidarity, the Jewish communists effectively prevent it from taking place. Their elation at their success is counterpointed by a quarrel within the Kahn family. Sarah, the mother, is strong and militant; Harry, the father, is an apathetic weakling who shies away from the dangers of street fighting to take refuge in his mother's flat.

Twenty years later, Sarah is still an active party member, but the others have dropped out of the fight. Aunt Cissie, formerly a trade union organizer, is living on her pension. Hymie is in business. Prince works in a secondhand shop. Dave is living with Ada in the country, making furniture. Monty, disillusioned by the Stalinist killings, has left the party. His wife is pregnant and he hopes that his greengrocer's business in Manchester will bring in enough to pay for a university education for his son.

In the play's final scene, Ronnie,* Sarah's son, comes home boiling over with indignation about the action of Soviet Russia in quelling the revolution in Hungary. All Sarah can say about it is that she too is hurt by what has happened. But then the focus shifts from public politics to her private need for political involvement—which Sarah equates with a need to fight the kind of apathy she associates with Harry. Under the pressure that has been built up by a highly theatrical argument, she tells Ronnie how Harry's weakness could literally have caused Ada's death. When she had diphtheria, while Sarah was pregnant with Ronnie, it was a neighbor who saved the child's life by giving her chicken soup with barley. Meanwhile Harry was seen spending his relief money at Bloom's, eating salt-beef sandwiches.

Although the play lacks a vivifying central image like *The Kitchen,* Wesker uses Sarah very effectively as a central figure, modulating between family squabbles and the wider arena in which she carries on her fight against apathy. In their

* Ronald is an anagram of Arnold.

repetitiveness, some of her rows with Harry have a curious affinity with the dialogue Pinter was writing in the same year (1957) in *The Room, The Dumb Waiter* and *The Birthday Party*. Though Pinter's characters are not Jewish, he, like Wesker, was the son of an East End Jewish tailor, and the dominating, nagging, working-class Jewish mother figure certainly seems to have inspired the dialogue of both playwrights.

> SARAH: What's the matter, you didn't have any tea by Lottie's?
> HARRY: No.
> SARAH: Liar!
> HARRY: I didn't have any tea by Lottie's, I tell you (*injured tone*). Good God, woman, why don't you believe me when I tell you things?
> SARAH: *You* tell *me* why. Why don't I believe him when he tells me things! As if he's such an angel and never tells lies. What's the matter, you never told lies before I don't think?
> HARRY: All right, so I had tea at Lottie's. There, you satisfied now?
> SARAH (*preparing things as she talks*): Well, of course you had tea at Lottie's. Don't I know you had tea at Lottie's? You think I'm going to think that Lottie wouldn't make you a cup of tea?
> HARRY: Oh, leave off, Sarah.
> SARAH: No! This time I won't leave off. (*Her logic again.*) I want to know why you told me you didn't have tea at Lottie's when you know perfectly well you did. I want to know.
> (*Harry raises his hands in despair.*)
> *I* know you had tea there and you know you had tea there—so what harm is it if you tell me? You think I care whether you had a cup of tea there or not? You can drink tea there till it comes out of your eyes and I wouldn't care only as long as you tell me.

The whole first act, like the first scene of *The Kitchen,* is very cleverly constructed, but it is a big disadvantage that the main action (the battle against the fascist marchers) occurs off stage. All we can get in the on-stage dialogue is a briefing in Scene One about the plan of campaign and then a narrative in Scene Two, when the battle is over, about what happened. One character who is in need of first aid for a head wound is on stage to bring some sign of the battle into the stage picture. Though much of the dialogue is inevitably about the battle, the characters are made very likable in their elation, the singing is well used to thicken the atmosphere, and Wesker adds in several neat theatrical touches—as when Monty sticks a feather into the bandage on the wounded head. But the climax that provides the curtain for Act One has nothing to do with the off-stage action. Harry has taken ten shillings out of Sarah's handbag, and both Ronnie and Ada are witnesses to the quarrel that ensues. The sudden switch from ferocious rage against her weakling husband to tenderness towards the children touchingly closes the act.

The second act presents the mid-stage in the general disillusionment with communism and in the break-up of the solidarity of the comrades. The fact that ten years have passed is planted neatly enough when Sarah complains:

> Ah, Harry, you couldn't even make money during the war. The war! When *everybody* made money.

And there is a warm, well-observed, brother-sister scene when Ronnie (now fifteen) teases Ada (now twenty-five) about the letters Dave is writing to her from the army. A theme is introduced here that will be central in *I'm Talking about Jerusalem*. Ada announces that when Dave comes back they will give up political activity and go to live in the country.

> ADA: I do not believe in the right to organize people. And anyway I'm not so sure that I love them enough to *want* to organize them.
> SARAH (*sadly*): This—from *you*, Ada? You used to be such an organizer.

ADA: I'm tired, mother. I spent eighteen months waiting
for Dave to return from Spain and now I've waited
six years for him to come home from a war against
Facism and I'm tired. Six years in and out of offices,
auditing books and working with young girls who are
morons—lipsticked, giggling morons. And Dave's experience is the same—fighting with men whom he
says did not know what the war was about. Away
from their wives they behaved like animals. In fact
they wanted to get away from their wives in order to
behave like animals. Give them another war and
they'd run back again. Oh yes! the service killed any
illusions Dave may have once had about the splendid
and heroic working class.

HARRY (*pedantically*): This is the talk of an intellectual,
Ada.

ADA: God in heaven save me from the claptrap of a
threepenny pamphlet. How many friends has the
Party lost because of lousy meaningless titles they
gave to people. *He* was a bourgeois intellectual, *he*
was a Trotskyist, *he* was a reactionary Social Democrat. Whisht! Gone!

HARRY: But wasn't it true? Didn't these people help to
bolster a rotten society?

ADA: The only rotten society is an industrial society. It
makes a man stand on his head and then convinces
him he is goodlooking. I'll tell you something. It wasn't
the Trotskyist or the Social Democrat who did the
damage. It was progress! There! Progress! And nobody dared fight progress.

SARAH: But that's no reason to run away. Life still carries on. A man gets married, doesn't he? He still has
children, he laughs, he finds things to make him
laugh. A man can always laugh, can't he?

ADA: As if that meant he lived? Even a flower can grow
in the jungle, can't it? Because there is always some
earth and water and sun. But there's still the jungle,
still the mad disorder of trees and fern, struggling for
its own existence, and the sick screeching of animals
terrified of each other. As if laughter were proof!

HARRY: And we and the Party don't want to do away
with the jungle, I suppose?

> ADA: No, you do not want to do away with the jungle, I suppose. You have *never* cried against the jungle of an industrial society. You've never wanted to destroy its *values*—simply to own them yourselves. It only seemed a crime to you that a man spent all his working hours in front of a machine because he did not own that machine. Heavens! the glory of owning a machine!

Interesting though this is as argument, it is too unrelated to the action, and the medium is not being used sufficiently in the explication of the situation which is being developed. It is only when the argument comes back to the subject of apathy, with Sarah blaming Ada's state of mind on Harry's influence, that the play becomes airborne again. The scene ends very theatrically as Harry has his first stroke.

One of the weaknesses of the trilogy is that it is not only in *Roots* that Ronnie is more effective in his absence than in his presence. And in the second scene in Act Two he is more interesting when he is reading a passage from Harry's abortive attempt at an autobiography than he is when he is making phrases in his own right.

> "Of me, the dummy and my family." . . . "Sitting at my work in the shop one day my attention was drawn to the dummy that we all try the work on. The rhythm of the machines and my constant looking at the dummy rocked me off in a kind of sleepy daze. And to my surprise the dummy began to take the shape of a human, it began to speak. Softly at first, so softly I could hardly hear it. And then louder and still louder, and it seemed to raise its eyebrows and with a challenge asked: your life, what of you life? My life? I had never thought, and I began to take my mind back, way back to the time when I was a little boy."*

* This is taken verbatim from an unfinished autobiography by Wesker's father, who filled two exercise books and then stopped.

Compare this with Ronnie's:

> I have all the world at my fingertips. Nothing is mixed
> up. I have so much life that I don't know who to give
> it to first. I see beyond the coloured curtains of *my*
> eyes to a world—say how do you like that line? Be-
> yond the coloured curtains of *my* eyes, waiting for a
> time and timing nothing but the slow hours, lay the
> thoughts in the mind. Past the pool of *my* smile . . .
>
> CISSIE: What does that mean?
> RONNIE: What, the pool of my smile? It's a metaphor—
> the pool of my smile—a very lovely metaphor.

Presumably Wesker does not agree that this is a very lovely
metaphor. Ronnie is intended to be a weak character. But,
except in *Roots*, we never know quite what attitude Wesker
wants us to adopt towards him, whereas characters like Sarah
and Cissie are very precisely defined by their dialogue. It
might be that an actor with great personal charm could save
Ronnie from seeming tiresome. But it would be very hard to
gain as much sympathy for him as he needs at the end of Act
Three when at the end of Act Two he behaves like this:

> RONNIE: What about me? (*He regards himself in a
> mirror.*) Young, good-looking, hopeful, talented . . .
> hopeful, anyway.
> SARAH (*sadly*): You? I'll wait and see what happens to
> you. Please God you don't make a mess of your life,
> please God. Did you ask for that rise?
> RONNIE: I did ask for that rise. "Mr. Randolph," I
> said—he's the manager of that branch—"Mr. Ran-
> dolph, I know that the less wages you pay us book-
> shop assistants the more you get in your salary. But
> don't you think I've sold enough books for long
> enough time to warrant you foregoing some of your
> commission?"
> SARAH: So what did he say, you liar?
> RONNIE: "You're our best salesman," he said, "but I've
> got to keep head office happy."

> SARAH: So what did you say, you liar?
>
> RONNIE: So I said, "It's not head office, it's your wife."
>
> SARAH: So what did he say, you liar?
>
> RONNIE: He said, "Kahn," he said, "as you're so frank and you know too much I'll give you a two pound rise."
>
> SARAH: Ronnie, did you get a rise, I asked you?
>
> RONNIE (*kissing her*): No.

Like the movements of the cooks in *The Kitchen*, the card game that the characters play in Act Three is meticulously worked out. By specifying how the cards fall and who takes which trick, Wesker builds a scaffolding from which he can construct the drama of family tensions which is played out in the bickering arguments.

> CISSIE: Thank you. Can I start now?
>
> SARAH: Is it your lead? I thought Prince dealt the cards.
>
> CISSIE: What's the matter with you, Sarah—Hymie dealt them.
>
> PRINCE: I could have sworn Sarah dealt them.
>
> CISSIE: Hymie, who dealt the cards?
>
> HYMIE: We've been so long deciding what to call that I don't know any more. Did I deal them? I don't remember.

And just as in *The Kitchen* a scream is sometimes used to interrupt the foreground action and widen the focus of the picture, here a scream from the playground below silences the card players and reminds us of life going on in the block of flats where last week a woman of thirty-two tried to kill herself. But, as in Act One, the talk about off-stage action neither makes up for the shortage of on-stage action nor has quite the right relationship to such action as is going on.

It is only when Ronnie returns, ten years older and disillusioned with what international communism has become, that the action becomes lively again. He is on fire to confront

Sarah with his indignation and though the only conflict between them is a verbal one, there is no lack of dramatic
tension in it. The only letdown comes with the language Ronnie uses, which is facile and rhetorical.

> Take me by the hand and show me who was right and
> who was wrong. Point them out. Do it *for* me. I stand
> here and a thousand different voices are murdering my
> mind.
> Were we cheated or did we cheat ourselves? I just
> don't know, God in heaven, I just do not know! Can
> you understand what it is suddenly not to know? (*col-
> lapses into armchair*) And the terrifying thing is—I
> don't care either.
> The family you always wanted has disintegrated, and
> the great ideal you always cherished has exploded in
> front of your eyes. But you won't face it. You just re-
> fuse to face it. I don't know how you do it but you do—
> you just do.

The language Wesker writes for Sarah is better, perhaps
because he is characterizing her more consistently. She is
further removed from himself.

> Philosophy? You want philosophy? Nothing means any-
> thing! There! Philosophy! I know! So? Nothing! Despair
> —die then! Will that be achievement? To die? (*softly*)
> You don't want to do that, Ronnie. So what if it all
> means nothing? When you know that you can start
> again. Please, Ronnie, don't let me finish this life think-
> ing I lived for nothing. We got through, didn't we? We
> got scars but we got through. You hear me, Ronnie?
> (*she clasps him and moans*). You've got to care, you've
> got to care or you'll die.

But moving though this final warning against apathy is, the
fusion between personal and political material is not working
well enough here to justify this apocalyptic ending. The only
way Sarah can be made to bridge between her own doubts

about Hungary and this degree of positiveness is by changing the subject to Harry and the way he ate salt-beef sandwiches in Bloom's instead of caring for his ailing daughter. For her, apathy is the great evil and political activity is the great good. For her, the inadequacy of the existing system is proved by its failure to help Harry.

Certainly, the line of argument Wesker gives Sarah serves very well to characterize the way her mind works. But he does not use it to characterize the way her mind works. He uses it to build up to a triumphant fanfare of positive feelings like Beatie's at the final curtain of *Roots,* and the placing of this note of affirmation implicitly claims such a general validity for the feeling that the flaws and confusions in the argument are forgotten. The fire in the emotional furnace is stoked so high that we sweat with agreement. Sarah must be right, and we go out of the theater determined, above all, to go on caring.

Roots

Compared with Albee . . . he looks like a theatrical primitive . . . *Roots* is written as if the author had just stumbled on John Galsworthy.

The most affecting last act in contemporary English drama . . . Among living playwrights Mr. Wesker has few peers when it comes to evoking an atmosphere of family cohesiveness.

These excerpts from Robert Brustein's and Kenneth Tynan's reviews of *Roots* show how two of the best drama critics have disagreed about it. In England, the consensus of critical opinion would be closer to Tynan's view of the play, but Brustein makes a good point about Wesker's main preoccupation:

His theme is not the ennobling of the masses, but their brutalization by mass culture; and, like John Osborne and Doris Lessing, he dramatizes the dilemma of the powerless intellectual, hungry for a social faith, but disillusioned by the failures of the preceding generation.

As a prophet who (unlike Tynan) has the courage to cry out against the dangers of pop culture and who gets a hearing for what he has to say, Wesker is extremely important.* The question is whether he will be remembered for his political, social and cultural activities and their influence, for his criticisms of society—which are valid but which fail to have influence—or for his plays.

One of my own difficulties in writing about him is that I admire his courage and outspokenness and agree with him about pop culture. I believe that such influence as he has in these matters is almost always a beneficial one and therefore it would seem logical to be in favor of his using every means at his disposal to get his criticisms across to the widest possible audience. But I also know that with the exception of *Chips with Everything* his plays suffer from the way he uses them to plug the message.

The argument about culture goes all the way through *Roots*. In part it is incorporated simply as argument and in part it is successfully dramatized. The basic idea of keeping Ronnie off the stage is brilliantly successful. He is more important in *Roots* than in either of the other plays, but his presence is created entirely through Beatie—partly through the way she quotes and mimicks him, but mainly through what she shows us of the influence he has had on her. She is in love, not just with him but with his whole way of life. So far as the plot is concerned, what matters is whether he will arrive and marry her; so far as the play is concerned, what matters is whether the gulf between his way of life and hers can possibly

* In his article, "Delusions of Floral Grandeur," published in *Envoy*, Wesker attacks the mystical pretensions of the Beatles and the cultural slumming of the intellectuals who have inherited a sense of guilt at enjoying opportunities which have been denied to the working classes. "And to offset their guilt the intellectuals desperately flirt with pop culture which they need to see as the 'tone of voice of the people,' while the pop singers, bewildered and intimidated by the adulation of the intellectual, feel the need to offset *their* guilt for having earned so much for, what they unconsciously despise as, so little, by flirting with what they imagine are intellectual concepts."

be bridged. This is why we need to see her against her family background. The quality she has in common with Ronnie is vitality. We know this without ever seeing them together. The main point is that although she was less than half alive until she met him, she does not come fully alive until the last five minutes of the play, when she is learning how to live without him. She has digested what he has to teach her and she is speaking with a voice of her own.

Although *Roots* makes this point very movingly and very theatrically, I do not think it makes it altogether successfully. But in leading up to it, the play broaches a number of fascinating questions. For example, how far can a self-educated urban intellectual influence an intelligent, uneducated, non-intellectual country girl? The cultural life of Beatie's family is measured against the yardstick of what Ronnie has taught Beatie: Mendelssohn and Bizet versus pop songs, books versus comics, art versus entertainment, discussion versus chatter, mental activity versus mental stagnation.

The conflict between the two ways of life surfaces in the argument about comics. When Beatie arrives at the house of her sister Jenny and her brother-in-law Jimmy, she starts reading a comic from a pile, and this reminds her of how angry Ronnie got when she used to read the comics he bought for his nephews.

> He used to get riled—
> (*Now Beatie begins to quote Ronnie, and when she does she imitates him so well in both manner and intonation that in fact, as the play progresses we see a picture of him through her.*)
> "Christ woman, what can they give you that you can *be* so absorbed?" So you know what I used to do? I used to get a copy of the *Manchester Guardian* and sit with that wide open—and a comic behind!
> JIMMY: *Manchester Guardian*? Blimey Joe—he don' believe in hevin' much fun then?
> BEATIE: That's what I used to tell him. "Fun?" he say,

"fun? Playing an instrument is fun, painting is fun, reading a book is fun, talking with friends is fun—but a comic? A comic? for a young woman of twenty-two?"

Jimmy is then made to scoff at people who enjoy books, paintings and classical music, and Beatie, shifting the conversation back from generalities to her personal experience, describes how Ronnie has helped her to get unemployment benefit. After standing up to the officials on her behalf, he has explained to her—rather pontifically,* we infer—that words are "bridges."

> "What can you talk of?" he'd ask. "Go on, pick a subject. Talk. Use the language. Do you know what language is?" Well, I'd never thought before—hev you?
> —it's automatic to you isn't it, like walking? "Well, language is words" he'd say, as though he were telling me a secret. "It's bridges, so that you can get safely from one place to another. And the more bridges you know about the more places you can see!" (*To Jimmy.*) And do *you* know what happens when you can see a place but you don't know where the bridge is?
> JIMMY (*angrily*): Blust gal, what the hell are you on about.
> BEATIE: Exactly! You see, you hev a row! Still, rows is alright. I like a row. So then he'd say: "Bridges! bridges! bridges! Use your bridges woman. It took thousands of years to build them, use them!" And that riled me. "Blust your bridges," I'd say. "Blust you and your bridges—I want a row." Then he'd grin at me. "You want a row?" he'd ask. "No bridges this time?" "No bridges," I'd say—and we'd row. Sometimes he hurt me but then, slowly he'd build the bridge up *for* me—and then we'd make love!

* Wesker has since told me that the intention was not to make Ronnie appear pontifical, but to emphasize his "playfulness"—his ability to enjoy reading, arguing and love-making in the same way.

After an argument about strikes and farm laborers and wages as compared with busmen's wages, culture is linked with politics when Beatie's challenges force Jimmy into expressing the countryman's resistance towards any attempt to change his life.

> You got a boy who's educated an' that and he's taught you a lot maybe. But don't you come pushin' ideas across at us—we're alright as we are. You can come when you like an' welcome but don't bring no discussion of politics in the house wi' you 'cos that'll only cause trouble. I'm telling you. (*He goes off.*)

This brings Beatie to acknowledge that there is a similar quality in her. Ronnie, who loves to discuss everything, encourages her to ask questions but, like her mother, she is often too stubborn to speak out. It is after this, in her simple, touching account of how she pursued Ronnie, that Beatie talks explicitly about Socialism on an intra-personal level.

> He was interested in all the things I never ever thought about. About politics and art and all that, and he tried to teach me. He's a socialist and he used to say you couldn't bring socialism to a country by making speeches, but perhaps you could pass it on to someone who was near you. So I pretended I was interested—but I didn't understand much. All the time he's trying to teach me but I can't take it Jenny.

Though much of this, inevitably, is worked out in terms of conversation, Beatie's proselytizing energy is also expressed in action when she makes Jenny tidy up her house. In a lively scene they drag out a muddy miscellany of clothes from the cupboard and fold them up.

In Act Two, in which Beatie is at her mother's house, the culture argument is resumed over a song. While Mrs. Bryant is peeling potatoes and Beatie is whipping the yolks of four eggs to make a cake—Wesker loves to get his characters cooking—she sings a folk song about a coalminer's wife. Mrs. Bryant indicates that she prefers "I'll wait for you in the heavens blue." When she admits that she does not know the words of the song, Beatie recites them for her, trying to demonstrate that they are third rate.

> Mrs. Bryant: Well alright, gal, so it's third-rate you say. Can you say why? What make that third rate and them frilly bits of opera and concert first rate? 'Sides, did I write that song? Beatie Bryant, you do go up and down in your spirits, and I don't know what's gotten into you gal, no I don't.
>
> Beatie: I don't know either, mother. I'm worried about Ronnie I suppose. I have that same row with him. I ask him exactly the same questions—what make a pop song third-rate. And he answer and I don't know what he talk about. Something about registers, something about commercial world blunting our responses. "Give yourself time woman," he say. "Time! You can't learn how to live overnight. *I* don't even know," he say, "and half the world don't know but we got to try. Try," he say, " 'cos we're still suffering from the shock of two world wars and we don't know it. Talk," he say, "and look and listen and think and ask questions." But Jesus! I don't know what questions to ask or *how* to talk.

As in *Chicken Soup with Barley*, personal and public issues, private life and generalized arguments are interwoven skillfully, though, in performance, there are passages where the characters are too transparently making the points which will carry Wesker's argument one stage further.

> Mrs. Bryant (*switching off radio*): Turn that squit off!
> Beatie (*turning on her mother violently*): mother! I could kill you when you do that. No wonder I don't know anything about anything. You give me nothing that was worthwhile, nothing. I never knowed any-

thing about the news because you always switched
off after the headlines. I never read any good books
'cos there was never any in the house. I never heard
nothing but dance music because you always turned
off the classics. I can't even speak English proper
because you never talked about anything important.

MRS. BRYANT: What's gotten into you now gal?

BEATIE: God in heaven mother, you live in the country
but you got no—no—no majesty. You spend your
time among green fields, you grow flowers and you
breathe fresh air and you got no majesty. You go on
and you go on talking and talking so your mind's
cluttered up with nothing and you shut out the world.
What kind of a life did you give me?

MRS. BRYANT: Blust gal, I weren't no teacher.

BEATIE: But you hindered. You din't open one door for
me. Even his mother cared more for me than what
you did. Beatie, she say, Beatie, why don't you take
up evening classes and learn something other than
waitressing. Yes, she say, you won't ever regret
learnin' things. But did you care what job I took up
or whether I learned things. You didn't even think it
was necessary.

Beatie here is spokesman for all the girls who have suffered
in the same way—most of them without realizing that they
were suffering, which makes their need for a spokesman all
the greater. But Beatie becomes less of an individual in talking
like this, and by giving so much valuable space to the argument, Wesker, who is perhaps the only playwright capable of
giving us a detailed and theatrically viable picture of how
farm laborers live in Norfolk, is throwing away his chance of
doing so. Knowing only too well that they do not spend their
time arguing about culture, we are left in ignorance about
how they do spend it. Admittedly, there are many incidents in
the play in which the central argument is bypassed, but the
play is shaped by this argument, and the other incidents seem
partly selected in order to provide contrast. The more Wesker
argues, the less he satisfies our appetite for documentary de-

tail. Instead of using Beatie's return to the country to contrast the life that goes on there with the life she has experienced in other places, Wesker makes her argue in generalized terms about the inarticulateness of all working-class girls, whether they live in the country or the town.

> It makes no difference country or town. *All* the town girls I ever worked with were just like me. It makes no difference country or town—that's squit. Do you know when I used to work at the holiday camp and I sat down with the other girls to write a letter we used to sit and discuss what we wrote about. An' we all agreed, all on us, that we started: "Just a few lines to let you know," and then we get on to the weather and then we get stuck so we write about each other and after a page an' half of big scrawl end up: "Hoping this finds you as well as it leaves me." There! We couldn't say any more. Thousands of things happening at this holiday camp and we couldn't find words for them. All of us the same.

In fact, of course, the two kinds of inarticulateness are rather different.

After this, Beatie tells her mother that she is going to teach her something. Placing a record on the phonograph, she plays Bizet's *L'Arlésienne Suite*. What she says echoes Ronnie's Culture = Socialism equation. Soon Beatie is actually dancing to the music.

> BEATIE: And now listen, listen, it goes together, the two tunes together, they knit, they're perfect. Don't it make you want to dance? (*She begins to dance a mixture of a cossack dance and a sailor's hornpipe.*)
> (*The music becomes fast and her spirits are young and high.*)
> Listen to that mother. Is it difficult? Is it squit? It's light. It make me feel light and confident and happy. God mother we could all be so much more alive and happy. Wheeeee. . . .

(*Beatie claps her hands and dances on and her Mother smiles and claps her hands and——*)

THE CURTAIN FALLS

With an actress of Joan Plowright's exuberance in the part, this produces a tremendously exciting curtain for Act Two. When the play was revived at the Royal Court in 1966, with another actress in the part, it was not exciting. It is easy enough to see Wesker's own exuberance behind the words, but he has not quite brought it into them.

In Act Three the argument is resumed in the form of a discussion about not having discussions in the family. Again, Wesker makes his characters play a game. Frank reads aloud a newspaper item about a boy who has been sentenced to six years in prison for assaulting an old lady. Mrs. Bryant says that if she were the judge she would have given him longer. Sticking a hat on her mother's head and an umbrella in her arms, Beatie challenges her to sum up as judge.

MRS. BRYANT: Well I—I—yes I—well I—Oh, don't be so soft.

FRANK: The mighty head is silent.

BEATIE: Well yes, she would be wouldn't she.

MRS. BRYANT: What do you mean, I would be? You don't expect me to *know* what they say in courts do you. I arn't no judge.

BEATIE: Then why do you say what you do? Suddenly —out of the blue—a judgement! You don't think about it. If someone do something wrong you don't stop and think why, you just sit and pass easy judgement. No discussin', no questions, just (*snap of fingers*)—off with his head. Look mother, when something go wrong in the family, do you ever sit and discuss it? I mean look at father getting less money. I don't see the family sittin' together and discussin' it. It's a problem! But which of you said it concerns you?

MRS. BRYANT: Nor don't it concern them. I aren't hevin' people mix in my matters.

BEATIE: But they aren't just people—they're your family for hell's sake!

MRS. BRYANT: No matters, I aren't hevin' it!

BEATIE: But mother I—

MRS. BRYANT: Now shut you up Beatie Bryant and leave it alone. I shall talk when I hev to and I never shall do so there!

Beatie then makes them play another game, asking them to decide which of five characters is morally the most guilty—a girl in love with a man on the other side of the river who does not love her, a wise man whose only advice is to do what she thinks best, a ferryman who will only take her across the river on condition that she strips, the man, who takes advantage of her nakedness or another man who has always said he loves her but now refuses to have anything to do with her. Most of the family refuse even to think about the moral problem, so Beatie tells them what Ronnie thinks and about the danger of not thinking.

Everyone must argue and think or they will stagnate and rot and the rot will spread.

It is immediately after this that the postman arrives with the letter announcing Ronnie's decision not to marry Beatie. Unlike the Kahns, who always discuss everything that concerns any one of them, the Bryants do not even try to help. And when she says she hates her mother, Beatie not only gets slapped across the face but gets the tables turned on her as well:

MRS. BRYANT: Go on—you say you know something we don't so *you* do the talking. Talk—go on, talk gal.

BEATIE (*despairingly*): I can't mother, you're right— the apple don't fall far from the tree do it? You're right, I'm like you. Stubborn, empty, wi' no tools for livin'. I got no roots in nothing. I come from a family o' farm labourers yet I ent got no roots—just like town people—just a mass o' nothin'.

This prepares the ground for Beatie's discovery that she *can* talk:

> BEATIE: Oh yes, we turn on a radio or a TV set maybe, or we go to the pictures—if them's love stories or gangsters—but isn't that the easiest way out? Anything so long as we don't have to make an effort. Well, am I right? You know I'm right. Education ent only books and music—it's asking questions, all the time. There are millions of us, all over the country and no one, not one of us is asking questions, we're all taking the easiest way out. Everyone I ever worked with took the easiest way out. We don't fight for anything, we're so mentally lazy we might as well be dead. Blust, we are dead! And you know what Ronnie say—it's our own bloody fault!
>
> JIMMY: So that's us summed up then—so we know where *we* are then!
>
> MRS. BRYANT: Well if he don't reckon we count nor nothin', then it's as well he didn't come. There! Its as well he didn't come.
>
> BEATIE: Oh, *he* thinks we count alright—living in mystic communion with nature. Living in mystic bloody communion with nature (indeed). But us count? Count mother? I wonder. Do we? Do you think we really count? You don' wanna take any notice of what them ole papers say about the workers bein' all important these days—that's all squit! 'Cos we aren't. Do you think when the really talented people in the country get to work they get to work for us? Hell if they do! Do you think they don't know we 'ont make the effort? The writers don't write thinkin' we can understand, nor the painters don't paint expecting us to be interested—that they don't, nor don't the composers give out music thinking we can appreciate it. "Blust," they say, "the masses is too stupid for us to come down to them. Blust," they say, "if they don't make no effort why should we bother?" So you know who come along? The slop singers and the pop writers and the film makers and women's magazines and the Sunday papers and the picture strip love

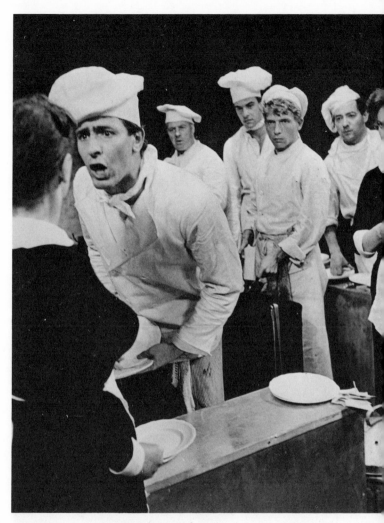

An explosive moment with Robert Stephens as PETER in the
Royal Court Theatre production of *The Kitchen*.
STUDIO EDMARK

Gwen Nelson as MRS. BRYANT and Bridget Turner as
BEATIE BRYANT in the 1967 revival of *Roots* at the Royal
Court Theatre.

The original 1962 London production of *Chips with Everything* was successfully transferred to Broadway the following year.

Ian McKellen as ANDREW COBHAM, the architect pro-
tagonist of *Their Very Own and Golden City*, at the Royal
Court Theatre.

Paul Roebling as ADAM and Barbara Haynes as BEATRICE
in *Four Seasons* at New York's Theatre Four in March 1968.
HENRY GROSSMAN

stories—that's who come along, and you don't have to make no effort for them, it come easy. "We know where the money lie," they say, "hell we do! The workers've got it so let's give them what they want. If they want slop songs and film idols we'll give 'em that then. If they want words of one syllable, we'll give 'em that then. If they want the third rate, BLUST! We'll give 'em THAT then. Anything's good enough for them 'cos they don't ask for no more!" The whole stinkin' commercial world insults us and we don't care a damn. Well, Ronnie's right—it's our own bloody fault. We want the third-rate—we got it! We got it! We got it! We . . .

(*Suddenly Beatie stops as if listening to herself. She pauses, turns with an ecstatic smile on her face ——*)

D'you hear that? D'you hear it? Did you listen to me? I'm talking. Jenny, Frankie, mother—I'm not quoting no more.

As Joan Plowright played this it was superbly effective but of course these are still Ronnie's opinions that Beatie is quoting and they are still too obviously Wesker's. This only matters in practice because it generalizes the dialogue away from Beatie's personal awareness of her personal pain. Even at the moment of being jilted, she is made to act as a spokesman and this prevents Wesker from focusing as he otherwise could have on the crucial question of how (and how far) Beatie is coming to life in her own right. He obviously wants us to accept her own assessment of the change that is taking place in her. But the evidence he gives us indicates that it is not entirely accurate. The points he wants to make through her are treated as more urgent than the personal drama.

What I have done so far has been to trace the development of the central argument. It is time to ask what I have left out in doing so.

I have ignored episodes like the death of Stan Mann, the neighbor. Like Harry Kahn, Stan becomes incontinent and after he has messed his trousers in the fields, Jimmy turns a hose on him to clean him up. This causes him to catch pneumonia and die. The comic disaster and the tragic result are all, of course, narrated at second hand, but they contribute usefully to the effectiveness of Stan Mann's appearances on stage. His lively dialogue gives a good impression of how lively he was in action when he was young and we get a strong feeling of how much his neighbors like him.

There are action episodes like the wasp-hunting Mrs. Bryant does with her daughter and the scene between Mr. Healey, a manager at the farm, and Mr. Bryant, who is a pigman. This corresponds to the scene in *I'm Talking about Jerusalem* in which the Colonel fires Dave. In both plays, the employer-exploiter is not given the same depth of sympathy that the other characters get. Wesker does well though not to make Mr. Bryant into a more sympathetic character in order to get more sympathy for him when he loses his job. He is a mean man who grudges Beatie the electricity it would use up to bake a cake for Jenny.

Wesker is not only interested in the way the minds of the farm laborers work, he is able to characterize it both through what they say and through the way they say it. Their slow rhythm of thinking is echoed in their slow and repetitious way of talking.

> JENNY: Now shut you up Jimmy Beales and get that food down you. Every time you talk, look, you miss a mouthful! That's why you complain of pain in your shoulder blades.
> BEATIE: You bin hevin' pains then Jimmy?
> JIMMY: Blust yes! Right a'tween my shoulder blades.
> JENNY: Mother says it's indigestion.
> BEATIE: What the hell's indigestion doin' a'tween his shoulder blades?
> JENNY: Mother reckon some people get indigestion so bad that it go right through their stomach to the back.
> BEATIE: Don't talk daft!

JENNY: That's what I say. Blust mother, I say, you don't git indigestion in the back. Don't you tell me, she say, I hed it.

BEATIE: What hevn't she hed.

If only he had been content to write a more documentary and less didactic play, he might have written a great play. I know, of course, that this statement is as whimsical as any of the other Ifs of history. If he were less didactic, he would not have the same kind of energy, and it is something that he succeeded in trapping so much of it into this powerful battery of a play.

I'm Talking about Jerusalem

In *Roots* there is only an interval of two days between Act One and Act Two and of two weeks between Act Two and Act Three. *I'm Talking about Jerusalem* is closer in method to *Chicken Soup with Barley,* with a gap of twelve months between the first act and the second, of six years between the two scenes in Act Two, a three-year gap before Act Three, Scene One, and another three-year gap before Scene Two. In subject, too, the play is closer to *Chicken Soup with Barley,* charting a process of disillusionment but focusing this time on a private experiment with political implications—Ada's and Dave's attempt to build a socialist life for themselves on William Morris lines. At first Dave works for the Colonel, who is a gentleman farmer, as a carpenter. After being fired, he tries to earn a living making furniture by hand. He fails and the last scene ends with their packing up to leave the cottage, just as the first scene began with their unpacking. The title sadly questions the possibility of building any such Jerusalem in England's green and pleasant land.

I'm Talking about Jerusalem is the least satisfying play in the trilogy—partly because of the unsatisfactoriness of the grown-up Ronnie, partly because of the loose construction, and partly because of the failure of the attempts at poetic moments. The most embarrassing is Ada's game with the off-stage child in Act Two.

DANNY: I shan't show myself until you play the game with me.

ADA: Oh! And what is the game today Daniel?

DANNY: It is called "Look I'm alive!"

(*Dave does a there-I-told-you-so look.*)

ADA: Oh that one. All right. Are you ready?

DANNY: Yes. Now you do it with me.

(*Now Ada faces us and goes through the same actions as we must assume Danny does. She starts crouched down, with her face hidden in her arm—as in the womb.*)

ADA: Are you crouched down?

DANNY (*in his own voice*): Yes Mummy.

(*Dave pulls a face at her so she draws him into the game too.*)

ADA: Do you mind if my friend here plays Mr. Life? (*Dave tries to run away.*) Dave!

DANNY: No, hurry up, I'm getting cramp.

(*What happens from now must have the touch of magic and of clowning. The day has gone and now the light fades slowly into evening.*)

DAVE (*bowing first to Ada, then to Danny*): I am— (*pauses to Ada*) what's it?

ADA: You're Mr. Life.

DAVE: Oh yes, Mr. Life. I am Mr. Life. I have spent all day making furniture and now I am going to make a human being. You are clay and I am going to make you into a human being. I am going to breathe the fire of life into you. Hissssss, Hissssss, Hissssss.

(*As Dave breathes the fire Ada unfolds and rises very slowly—this is what Danny is doing unseen—her eyes are closed.*)

DAVE: Now you have life and you can breathe.

(*Ada breathes deeply.*)

DAVE: Now I will give you sight.

(*He snaps his fingers at Danny then at Ada. Ada opens her eyes. There is wonder and joy at what is revealed.*)

DAVE: Now I will give you movement.
> (*Dave beckons to Danny then to Ada. Ada raises and lowers her arms twice, moving her head from left to right at the same time, full of curiosity and excitement at what she is doing.*)

DAVE: Now I will give you speech. (*He draws something unseen from his mouth and throws it to Danny, then he kisses his finger and places the kiss on Ada's lips.*) Tell me, what does it feel like to be a human being?

DANNY (*in his gruff voice*): It's a little strange. But I'm getting used to it. It's very exciting.

Wesker is always at his worst when he makes his characters play games but this one, in its conscious striving after charm, is rather like Dave's conversation with the unborn Danny in Act Two, Scene One.

> DAVE: I tell you he's talking. Yes. Yes, I can hear you—sounds like a dozen drains emptying—what's that? You don't want to come out? But you've got to come out, I don't care how comfortable it is you'll get cramp. No I'm not going to send a bloody taxi for you—you'll walk. Now you listen to me, you come out when you're told or I'll plug you in there for life—you hear me?

Both passages are much worse than the game Beatie plays in *Roots* making her mother into a judge or the rather similar game that Ronnie tries to play at the beginning of Act One with the removal men—furniture movers—who seem surprised that anyone should want to live here:

> Come on, Dave. Give them an answer. It's a golden opportunity this. The world has asked you why you've come here. There stands the world (*to R. Men*) and here stand you two. You're on trial comrade.
> ADA: Don't arse around Ronnie, the men want their tea.
> RONNIE: But I'm serious, girl. I want to know too.

> You've always been my heroes, now you've changed
> course. You've left communism behind—what now?

These games are intended merely as justification for opening
the throttle on the argument and they betray an uneasiness at
writing too expositorily.

The writing of Ronnie's part now makes even heavier demands on the actor's personality, with an awkward blend of
high seriousness and arch skittishness. When the curtain goes
up, a portable radio is playing Beethoven's Ninth Symphony
and Ronnie is standing on a box, conducting and telling the
removal men what to do. Sarah, who all through the play is
muted, compared with what she was in *Chicken Soup with
Barley*, is often used just as a foil to Ronnie. When he recites
some poetry by Louis MacNeice which he says he would like
to have written, Sarah, thinking it is Ronnie's own poetry,
tells him he ought to be able to get it published. Much of
Ronnie's boisterous clowning at the beginning has the look of
being written in to give relief to the plains of exposition; but
sheer bustling activity is no substitute for action, and the main
action of Act One—coming to live in the country—is already
complete before the curtain goes up. What remains to be
worked out through dialogue is the significance of the move.
In Sarah's view, Ada and Dave are running away from socialism to an ivory tower. For Dave it is an experiment in socialism on the level of personal and family relationships. But his
condemnation of factory life can only be a verbal one. It also
contains a lot of hollow rhetoric:

> Since being demobbed I've worked in a factory turning
> out doors and window frames and I've seen men hating
> themselves while they were doing it. Morning after
> morning they've come in with a cold hatred in their eyes,
> brutalized! All their humanity gone. These you call men?
> All their life they're going to drain their energy into
> something that will give them nothing in return. . . .
> In a year's time that barn'll be my workshop. There I

shall work and here, ten yards from me, where I can see and hear them, will be my family. And they will share in my work and I shall share in their lives. I don't want to be married to strangers. I've seen the city make strangers of husbands and wives, but not me, not me and my wife.

The first dramatic and touching moment comes nearly at the end of Act One when Sarah shows how personally she is taking what Dave and Ada are doing. She thinks that Dave is taking her daughter away from her because he dislikes her. But the family squabble which follows after a scene with the Colonel remains too much like a private joke: Ronnie sits down to eat in his raincoat and despite protests from the others refuses to take it off until Sarah mocks him by sitting at the table with her umbrella up.

The structure of Act Two is rather crude. First there is an awkward build-up for the entrance of Libby Dobson, who is now staying with Dave and Ada, and then, after the conversation about the unborn baby, there is an awkward build-up to the climax of the scene in which the Colonel is to fire Dave. Noticing the rolls of linoleum outside the cottage, Ada asks what they are. Dave first says that the Colonel threw them away and then that he left them lying around in the shed for months. Trouble, obviously, is brewing.

Most of the space in this scene is devoted to the dialogue with Libby, an embittered ex-socialist who has made a socialist experiment of his own, which parallels Ada's and Dave's. Naturally, it can only be described in retrospective narrative:

> I've tried it, Dave—listen to me and go home—I've tried it and failed. Socialism? I didn't sell out that easily. You've gone back to William Morris, but I went back to old Robert Owen. Five thousand pound my old man left me, and I blushed when I heard it. But I still hung on. It's not mine, I decided—the profits of exploitation, I said. Right! Give it back! So I worked out a plan. I

found four other young men who were bright mechanics like myself and who were wasting their talents earning ten pounds a week in other men's garages, and I said "Here's a thousand pounds for each of you—no strings, no loans, it's yours! Now let's open our own garage and exploit no one but ourselves. There's only one provision," I said, "only one: as soon as there is an excess profit of another thousand pounds, we find someone else to inherit it and we expand that way!" See the plan? A chain of garages owned and run by the workers themselves, the real thing, and I will build it myself. Can you imagine what a bloody fool they must have thought me? Can you guess the hell of a time they had planning to buy me out? Democracy, mate? I spit it! Benevolent dictatorship for me. You want Jerusalem? Order it with an iron hand—no questions, no speeches for and against—bang! It's there! You don't understand it? You don't want it? Tough luck, comrade—your children will! (*To Ada*) No peace? You're right, Mrs. Simmonds. I'm dirtied up. Listen to me, Dave, and go home before you're dirtied up.

This is followed by another even longer narrative from Libby about his wife and how he had to watch her growing fatter and more slovenly and more acquisitive just at the time when he was going back to the principles of Robert Owen.

The six-year gap between the two scenes in Act Two necessitates some complex exposition at the beginning of the second scene. Dave has now converted the barn into a workshop for making furniture. He has an apprentice. A customer is on his way over to see a chair he has ordered, Ada is due back from London and Harry has had his second stroke. After all this the scene settles down to an argument between Dave and his apprentice about factory work versus craftsmanship and the freedom of being part of a small unit.

Look Sammy, look at this rack you made for your chisels. Not an ordinary rack, not just bits of wood nailed together, but a special one with dove-tail joints here and mortise and tenon joint there, and look what you put on the side, remember you wanted to decorate it, so you used my carving tools and you worked out a design. For no reason at all you worked out a design on an ordinary chisel rack. But there was a reason really wasn't there? You enjoyed using those tools and making up that design. I can remember watching you—a whole afternoon you spent on it and you used up three pieces of oak before you were satisfied. Twenty-seven and six you owe me.

SAMMY: Hell, that were only messing around.

DAVE: *Not* messing around. Creating! For the sheer enjoyment of it just creating. And what about the fun we had putting up this workshop?

SAMMY: It's not that I don't enjoy myself Dave.

DAVE: But that's not all cocker. It's not only the fun or the work—it's the place. Look at it, the place where we work. The sun reaches us, we get black in the summer. And any time we're fed up we pack up and go swimming. Don't you realize what that means? There's no one climbing on our backs. Free agents Sammy boy, we enjoy our work, we like ourselves.

SAMMY: You think I don't know these things, hell Dave. But I've seen the boys in the village, I know them, they don't care about things and I see them hang around all their lives, with twopence halfpenny between them an' half a dozen dependants. But I want to get on—don't you think I ought to get on?

DAVE: A bait! A trap! Don't take any notice of that clap-trap for God's sake boy. For every hundred that are lured only one makes it. One, only one. Factories? Offices? When you're in those mate you're there for good.

They are interrupted by Ada's return from London and the news she brings of another off-stage event. Harry's second stroke has affected his brain and he is in a padded cell.

Three years later (Act Three, Scene One) the aunts come down on a visit and their conversation is allowed to dominate the scene. They report on the progress of the Ronnie-Beatie affair and they provide a mildly amusing diversion by describing how Ronnie, in cooking rice for them, forgot how cooking swelled it and ended up with seven pans full of rice for three people. Too much of the dialogue fails to bear either directly or indirectly on the real subject of the scene, which is that the failure of Dave's experiment is becoming obvious. The aunts want to discuss why Dave and Ada no longer want to discuss their problems with them, and again this discussion about discussion is made into a cue for explicitness—this time in the form of an outburst:

> Once and for all I'll tell you—you call me a prophet and laugh do you? Well, I'll tell you. I *am* a prophet. Me. No one's ever heard of me and no one wants to buy my furniture but I'm a bleedin' prophet and don't anyone forget that. As little as you see me so big I am. Now you look at me. I picked up my spear and I've stuck it deep. Prophet Dave Simmonds, me. With a chisel. Dave Simmonds and Jesus Christ. Two yiddisha boys——
>
> ESTHER: Hatred, Cissie. Look at our nephew-in-law, hatred in every spit.
>
> DAVE: Well, what have you left me for God's sake? You want an angel in me? Ten years I spent here trying to carve out a satisfactory life for my wife and kids and on every side we've had opposition. From the cynics, the locals, the family. Everyone was choking with their experience of life and wanted to hand it on. Who came forward with a word of encouragement? Who said we maybe had a little guts? Who offered one tiny word of praise?

The final scene is set against the background of the Conservative victory of 1959. They are listening to the election results as Sarah and Ronnie are helping them to pack and Ronnie gives us his version of the Beatie affair:

> You know what my father once said to me? "You can't change people Ronnie," he said, "you can only

give them some love and hope they'll take it." Well
Beatie Bryant took it but nothing seemed to happen.

DAVE: Three years is a long time to go with a girl.

RONNIE: I don't regret it. Maybe something did happen.
After all little Sarah, wasn't it you who was always
telling us that you don't know people without something happening?

SARAH: I'm always telling you you can't change the
world on your own—only no one listens to me.

RONNIE: We carry bits and pieces of each other, like
shrapnel from a war. Ada's like you Sarah, strong!
I'm charming, like my father, and weak. O God!
Isn't it all terribly, terribly sad.

Though it does not consciously aspire to a Chekhovian
tone, the ending tries to contrive a poetic dying fall out of
packing cases and abrupt mood changes at the moment of
quitting a home. But despite the emotional *non sequiturs,*
there is too much direct statement of emotion and too much
explication of the main themes. After Ronnie has done an Al
Jolson act, jumping up on a crate to sing a song, this follows:

RONNIE: I'm crying, Dave, I'm bloody crying.
    (*Everyone is unnerved. Everyone is feeling the
    reality of leaving. A long pained silence.*)

DAVE: So? We're all crying. But what do you want of
us. Miracles?

SARAH: I don't know what's happened to you all. Suddenly you're talking and then you're shouting and
then you're crying. Suddenly you start hitting each
other with words.

DAVE: Well, why must he put us on pedestals.

SARAH: You were the God that fought in Spain, Dave,
remember?

DAVE (*to Ronnie*): Is that it? (*Pause.*) You can't really
forgive me because I didn't speak heroically about
Spain, can you?

RONNIE (*reflectively*): The war that was every man's
war.

DAVE: A useless, useless bloody war because Hitler still

made it didn't he, eh? And out went six million Jews in little puffs of smoke. Am I expected to live in the glory of the nineteen thirties all my life?

SARAH: Sick! . . . You're all sick or something. We won the last war didn't we? You forgotten that? We put a Labour Party in power and . . .

RONNIE (*with irony*): Oh, yes, that's right! We put a Labour Party in power. Glory! Hurrah! It wasn't such a useless war after all, was it, Mother? But what did the bleeders do, eh? They sang the Red Flag in Parliament and then started building atom bombs. Lunatics! Raving lunatics! And a whole generation of us laid down our arms and retreated into ourselves, a whole generation! But you two. I don't understand what happened to you two. I used to watch you and boast about you. Well, thank God, I thought, it works! But look at us now, now it's all of us.

But none of this is dramatically substantiated. We never really come to see how important Dave and Ada are for Ronnie and his condemnation of the Labour Party is purely verbal. No dramatic resolution can be achieved this way. At the end it is not only Ronnie who is desperate to hit on a positive note, it is also Wesker.

DAVE (*angrily*): *Don't* moan at me about visions. Don't you know they don't work? You child you—visions don't work.

RONNIE (*desperately*): They *do* work! And even if they don't work then for God's sake let's try and behave as though they do—or else nothing will work.

But this is weak and so is the curtain:

ADA (*to Sarah and Ronnie*): Come on, you two, the men are waiting.
(*They have gone off by now. Ronnie has locked the door and Sarah is waiting for him. He takes one of the baskets from her and puts an arm on her shoulder.*)

RONNIE: Well Sarah—your children are coming home now.

SARAH: You finished crying, you fool you?

RONNIE: Cry? We must be bloody mad to cry, Mother. (*Sarah goes off leaving Ronnie to linger and glance once more around. Suddenly his eye catches a stone, which he picks up and throws high into the air. He watches, and waits till it falls. Then he cups his hands to his mouth and yells to the sky with bitterness and some venom—*) . . . .

RONNIE: We—must—be—bloody—mad—to cry!

(*The stage is empty.*

Soon we hear the sound of the lorry revving up and moving off.

A last silence.

Then——)

A LAST SLOW CURTAIN

Chips with Everything

In *Chips with Everything*, Wesker takes a re-
markable stride forward. As in *The Kitchen*, he is concerned
with a very large group of characters but he moves deftly
from one locale to another, concerning himself sometimes
with individuals in the foreground, sometimes with the group
as a whole, and using a Brechtian technique: each of the
short scenes is more or less capable of standing up dramatically, independently of the others. What is more important is
that the argument is not communicated explicitly through the
dialogue but through the sequence of actions. Most important
of all, Wesker is using language with a new assurance, economy and incisiveness. Instead of striving after poetic moments, he infuses a much more genuine poetry into dialogue
which is not at all "poetic," even finding gold in the alloy of
RAF speech, refining it as he reproduces it:

> But I will tear and mercilessly scratch the scorching
> day-lights out of anyone who smarts the alec with me—

and we've got some 'ere. I can see them, you can tell them.

He is now far better able to take his own talent as a mimic for granted, and while retaining what he needs of natural speech rhythms, he feels free to depart completely from realistic dialogue without departing too far from documentary accuracy. Characters are made unnaturalistically conscious of the way they themselves think so that they can speak out the sub-text of their thoughts:

> It's not that I want rigid men, I want clean men. It so happens, however, that you cannot have clean men without rigid men, and cleanliness requires smartness and ceremony.
> I want your body awake and ringing. Do you hear that? I want you so light on your feet that the smoke from a cigarette can blow you away, and yet so strong that you stand firm before hurricanes. I hate thin men and detest fat ones. I want you like Greek gods. You heard of the Greeks?

Sometimes Wesker carries the process too far, as he does with the Wing Commander:

> Civilians! How I hate civilians. They don't know—what do they know? How to make money, how to chase girls and kill old women. No order, no purpose. Conscripts! They bring their muddled lives and they poison us, Jack; they poison me with their indifference, and all we do is guard their fat bellies. I'd sacrifice a million of them for the grace of a Javelin Fighter, you know that?

But the stylization and the economy of the action, which builds up a pressure by telescoping the scenes and the episodes tightly together, justify most of the writing.

As in *The Kitchen*, Wesker is making his group of characters into a microcosm of our social and economic system. But the fact that National Servicemen, unlike cooks, are not free to leave, helps him to say what he has to say about oppression and social conditioning. Because of their clear-cut division of personnel into officers and men—and their rigid hierarchy which subdivides both categories into ranks—the armed services have often been used before as an image of society, but *Chips with Everything* embodies a more serious, powerful and systematic attack on the class system than any other play I know.

It starts, aptly, by showing how the habit of servile conformism is inculcated. Discipline is used to check down the liveliness and the individuality of individuals. The Air Force needs to de-individualize them into a group which will respond with mechanical obedience to orders. This is why drill is such an important feature of recruit training. We see nine recruits in a hut with a Drill Instructor who tries alternately to terrorize them into submission and to appeal to their good nature from what is left of his own. He comes from the working classes himself, but his technique of trying to gain power over his men by promising them hell if they resist and a good time if they conform is very much like the technique the officers adopt with Pip, the hero, who soon shows that he has the qualities of leadership. At first he inspires the other recruits to resist authority. Later he sells out and becomes an officer himself. This, Wesker is implicitly saying, is what so often happens in Britain or in any society governed by a hierarchy. The leader remains faithful only to his own talent for leadership, not to the masses who need to be led. The theme of the revolutionary who becomes an authoritarian has been treated effectively by writers like Koestler (especially in *The Gladiators*) and Camus (especially, in non-fictional terms, in *L'Homme Révolté*), but Wesker's treatment of the theme is both the clearest theatrical adumbration of the process and the most relevant to the current situation in Britain, where there are even writers (like John Osborne and Kingsley Amis) who are open to the charge of having gone over to the Establishment after starting off as rebels against it.

One question, though, that needs to be answered about *Chips with Everything* is whether the part of the play that deals with Pip's corruption by the officers is as good as the part in which he encourages the other recruits to resist them. It is time to look at both parts more closely.

Pip first stands out from the group in Scene Two, the Naafi [service canteen] scene. When Wilfe imitates his upper-class accent, he shows that it is not easy to make him either ashamed or afraid. He arouses the curiosity of the others because, though his father is a banker who has been a general, he does not want to become an officer himself. His only explanation is an indirect one—an account of meeting a working-class man at close quarters in an East End cafe:

> Then a man came and sat next to me—WHY should I have been surprised? I'd seen his face before, a hundred times on the front pages. of papers reporting a strike. A market man, a porter, or a docker. No, he was too old to be a docker. His eyes kept watering, and each time they did that he'd take out a neatly folded handker-chief, unfold it and, with one corner, he'd wipe away the moisture, and then he'd neatly fold it up again and replace it in his pocket. Four times he did that, and each time he did it he looked at me and smiled. I could see grains of dirt in the lines of his face, and he wore an old waistcoat with pearl buttons. He wasn't untidy, the cloth even seemed a good cloth, and though his hair was thick with oil it was clean. I can even remember the colour of the walls, a pastel pink on the top half and turquoise blue on the bottom, peeling. Peeling in fifteen different places; actually I counted them. But what I couldn't understand was why I should have been so surprised. It wasn't as though I had been cradled in my childhood. And then I saw the menu, stained with tea and beautifully written by a foreign hand, and on

top it said—God I hated that old man—it said "Chips with everything." Chips with every damn thing. You breed babies and you eat chips with everything.

In Scene Six, a leisurely evening scene in the hut, he shows his prowess as a spellbinding storyteller by getting them all interested in the French Revolution and in his family history. But it is in the next scene, at the Christmas Eve party in the Naafi, that he comes out into the open as an opponent of the hierarchical system that keeps the lower classes down low and conditions them into behaving as their social overlords expect them to behave. Wesker demonstrates this skillfully through the Wing Commander's patronizing attempt to organize an impromptu talent show. He expects the airmen to sing pop songs. Instead Pip persuades one boy to recite verse* and then drums the others into singing *The Cutty Wren,* an old peasant revolt song. In John Dexter's production, this built up superbly. Started off by a spoon tapped against a bottle, the rhythm got a hold on them all and gradually they joined in, expressing their defiance of the officers by singing out, stamping, clapping, thumping on the tables. The Wing Commander, knowing that war has been declared, tries to isolate Pip from the men whose battle he is fighting.

> WING COMMANDER: Quite the little leader, aren't you, Thompson? Come over here, I want a word with you in private. Stand to attention, do your button up, raise your chin—at ease. Why are you fighting me, Thompson? We come from the same side, don't we? I don't understand your reasons, boy—and what's more you're insolent. I have every intention of writing to your father.
> PIP: Please do.
> WING COMMANDER: Oh, come now. Listen, lad, per-

---

* He announces it as a poem by Burns, but what he recites is actually the anonymous seventeenth-century dirge called *A Lyke-Wake Dirge.*

haps you've got a fight on with your father or something, well that's all right by me, we all fight our
fathers, and when we fight them we also fight what
they stand for. Am I right? Of course I'm right. I
understand you, boy, and you mustn't think I'm un-
sympathetic. But it's not often we get your mettle
among conscripts—we need you. Let your time here
be a truce, eh? Answer me, boy, my guns are lowered
and I'm waiting for an answer.

The next scene, between Pip and Charles, shows how
difficult it is to make friends across the class barrier, and the
next, a scene in the hut, which has run out of coke for the
stove, leaves Pip out of the foreground till he comes forward
with the idea of stealing coke. The corporal makes it sound
difficult:

You think you'll get in the coke yard? You won't you
know, mate; there's a wire netting and a patrol on that.

We then see how Pip leads a successful raid on the yard. As
in *The Kitchen,* Wesker's stage directions lay down meticu-
lous guidelines for an action scene which is theatrically very
exciting when it moves fast.

*Ginger dashes to wire, and places chair—dashes
to other side of stage. Pip runs to chair, jumps up
and over. Dodger runs to take chair away and
joins Ginger. The Guard appears and carries on
round. Dodger runs back, places chair. Wilfe runs
to chair with another, jumps on it, and drops chair
into Pip's hands, runs off. Dodger runs on, and
withdraws chair. The Guard appears, and continues. Dodger runs on with chair again. Andrew runs
with buckets to chair, jumps up and passes them
to Pip. Ginger runs to take chair away. Guard
appears, and continues. In like process, two buckets
are returned "full" of coke. In the last stage,
Pip jumps back over netting, leaving chair. Ginger*

> *and Dodger appear with two stools. Dickey dashes
> on top of two stools, leans over wire and reaches
> down for chair, which he throws to Andrew.
> Dodger and Ginger run off with two stools. Guard
> appears, and continues. This scene can be, and has
> to be silent, precise, breathtaking, and finally very
> funny.*

The final scene in the act raises the question of whether they could have managed without Pip's leadership or whether leaders will always be necessary. He denies this.

> Your great-great-grandfather said there'll always be
> horses, your great-grandfather said there'll always be
> slaves, you grandfather said there'll always be poverty
> and your father said there'll always be wars. Each time
> you say "always" the world takes two steps backwards
> and stops bothering.

Saying "always," in other words, is a sign of the same sort of apathy and lethargy which have been embodied by Harry in *Chicken Soup with Barley*. Saying "always" is an alternative to taking action.

Act Two starts with a guard rousing the sleeping billet of airmen back from their Christmas leave. The Corporal then warns them of trouble ahead. The officers are gunning for Pip and he himself is gunning for three of the airmen: Smiler who annoys him because he always looks as though he is grinning, and two of the others that he thinks are troublemakers—Wilfe and Cannibal. There is a strongly threatening undertone in the scene of rifle drill which follows, and the Corporal's speech is splendidly contrived to depart from its basis of accurate mimicry of the Drill Instructor's idiom into something that goes very much deeper. But the actual point of departure, which comes at the middle of this passage, is not easy to detect:

> The first thing is—not to be afraid of it. It won't hurt
> you and if you handle it correctly you can't hurt it.

(*Only one boy laughs.*) I know you think they're nice, boys. With one of them in your hand you feel different, don't you, you feel a man, a conquering bloody hero? You want to run home and show your girl, don't you? Well, they're not toys—you can kill a man wi' one o' them. Kill 'im! Your napkins are still wet—you don't really understand that word "kill," do you? Well, you can be killed. There! Does that bring it home to you? A bullet can whip through your flesh and knock breath out of *you*. Imagine yourself dying, knowing you're dying, you can feel the hole in your body, you can feel yourself going dizzy, you can feel the hot blood, and you can't breathe. You want to breathe but you can't, the body you've relied on all these years doesn't do what you want it to do, and you can't understand it. You're surprised, you're helpless, like those dreams where you're falling—only dying isn't a dream because you know, you know, you know that you're looking at everything for the last time and you can't do a bloody thing about it, that's dying. And that's a rifle. So don't let me catch anybody aiming it at anybody—loaded or not.

The next scene shows two corporals threatening to "break" Smiler, who is up on charges because he clicked a trigger when his corporal told him not to; the following scene shows the officers trying to break Pip, who has applied for the menial RAF job of Administration Orderly.

PILOT OFFICER: Let's drop the pretence. We're the same age and class, let's drop this formal nonsense. The Air Force is no place to carry on a family war, Pip. This is not a public school, it's a place where old boys grow into young men, believe me. Don't force me to start listing all your virtues and attributes. We're not flattterers, but don't let's be falsely modest either—that's understood between us, I'm sure. God, when I think of what I did to try and get out of coming into this outfit—two years wasted I thought. But waste is what you yourself do with time—come on man, if people like us aren't officers, then imagine the bastards they'll get. This is a silly game, Pip—why look, you're even sulking. Admin orderly! Can you see yourself washing dishes?

Pip is not vulnerable to arguments like this. The tactics of the Wing Commander are much cleverer. He tells the Corporal that the standard in his squad is low, and the Corporal immediately starts tightening the discipline. The battle is on. Stylized passages of interlocution with the officers are alternated with squad scenes. At bayonet practice, Pip refuses to attack the dummy with his bayonet, and the Corporal puts him up on charges. He loses the support of the others, and the Pilot Officer, who is the key figure in the inquisition against him, now questions his motives:

> Comradeship? Not that, not because of the affinity of one human being to another, not that. Guilt? Shame because of your fellow being's suffering? You don't feel that either. Not guilt. An inferiority complex, a feeling of modesty? My God. Not that either. There's nothing humble about you, is there? Thompson, you wanted to do more than simply share the joy of imparting knowledge to your friends; no, not modesty. Not that. What then? What if not those things, my lad? You and I? Shall I say it? Power. Power, isn't it? Among your own people there were too many who were powerful, the competition was too great, but here, among lesser men —here among the yobs, among the good-natured yobs, you could be king.

This scene is followed immediately by another bayonet practice scene. This time Pip obeys the order to attack.

In performance it is hard to see exactly what has broken his resistance. This is how Wesker has explained the point in a letter to the American critic Harold Ribalow:*

* I am grateful to Arnold Wesker for showing it to me and allowing me to quote it.

You point out that "The Pilot Officer probes Thompson's mind and reveals it, both to Pip Thompson and to the audience." But in fact he is doing something subtler than that. He is corrupting Pip and I employ my own special definition of "corrupt" in this sense, *i.e.*, to corrupt is to present sensitive people with motives that they *could* have but haven't really, but which they are *persuaded* they have and in this way their confidence is undermined and they are argued out of action. In other words, Pip was not really concerned with power but he is tricked into believing he was.

In the next scene we see Charles, who still wants to be Pip's friend, asking him to teach him. The Pip of Act One would have responded to such a challenging request. Pip now refuses, but it is difficult to tell whether Wesker thinks that he deserves Charles's reproach—

> CHARLES: You lead and then you run away. I could grow with you, don't you understand that? We could do things together. You've got to be with someone, there's got to be someone you can trust, everyone finds someone and I found you—I've never asked anyone before, Jesus, never——
>
> PIP: Ask someone else.
>
> CHARLES: Someone else. Someone else. It's always someone else, you half-bake you, you lousy word-user you. Your bleedin' stuffed grandfathers kept us stupid all this time, and now you come along with your pretty words and tell us to fend for ourselves——

or whether he is trying to show Charles that one master is as bad as another:

> PIP: We'll do anything they want just because they know how to smile at us.
>
> CHARLES: You mean *I'll* do what they want, not you boy. You're one of them—you're just playing games with 'em, and us mugs is in the middle—I've cottoned

> on now. (*Long pause*). I'll do what *you* want, Pip.
> PIP: Swop masters? You're a fool, Charles, the kind of
> fool my parents fed on, you're a fool, a fool——

Possibly Wesker thinks that both points are valid, but in these two scenes the dramatic elisions are interfering with clarity.

We now cut to a scene which is very difficult to stage—a solo scene for Smiler, who has run away from the camp. A crescendo of the voices of persecuting corporals is relayed over the loudspeakers so that we hear what Smiler is hearing inside his head. This cues a hysterical monologue which shows that he has almost literally been broken:

> They think they own you——Oh my back. I don't
> give tuppence what you say, you don't mean anything
> to me, your bloody orders nor your stripes nor your
> jankers nor your wars. Stick your jankers on the wall,
> stuff yourselves, go away and stuff yourselves, stuff
> your rotten stupid selves—Ohh—Ohhh. Look at the sky,
> look at the moon, Jesus look at that moon and the frost
> in the air. I'll wait. I'll get a lift in a second or two, it's
> quiet now, their noise is gone. I'll stand and wait and
> look at that moon. What are you made of, tell me? I
> don't know what you're made of, you go on and on.
> What grouses you? What makes you scream? You're
> blood and wind like all of us, what grouses you? You
> poor duff bastards, where are your mothers?

He goes back to the camp and in the following scene we see him in the hut with the others. It is New Year's Eve. The others are preparing for their passing out parade—a ceremony that precedes their departure from recruit camp. They put the exhausted Smiler to bed, and when the Pilot Officer appears to take him to the guard room they resist passively, sitting down on their beds, one by one, instead of obeying the order to come to attention. Pip at first seems to side with them, but during a long speech in which he says Smiler has been badly treated and the boys are right, he is changing into an officer's uniform. At the end of the speech the Pilot Officer gives Pip a list from which he reads out their assignments and calls them to attention. Six of them are made Administration Orderlies, one is sent to a typing pool, and Smiler is made to do three extra weeks of recruit training. The final scene shows the passing out parade, and at the end the National Anthem is played with the audience still sitting down.

Pip's volte-face is theatrically most effective but the stylization and telescoping that worked so well in the earlier parts of the play are being overused here. Nevertheless, Wesker comes very close to resolving his argument successfully in theatrical terms, and the play, which is more ambitious than any of his earlier plays, is also better thought out, better constructed, and better written.

Their Very Own and Golden City

In a sense *Their Very Own and Golden City* is a development of the central theme of *Chips with Everything*—the relationship between the rebel and the Establishment, which tries to win him over. Andrew Cobham, the architect hero, is not corrupted to the same degree that Pip is corrupted. His ideal is to build six Golden Cities, cities to be owned and paid for by the people who live in them, cities to set a new pattern in cooperative socialism which would be imitated all over the world. He does not succeed, but he does not wholly fail. He does fail—as Wesker failed over Centre 42—to get more than token support from the T.U.C. So he compromises. He accepts the help of a Conservative Minister of Town and Country Planning, and in this way he does get one Golden City built.

It is an inordinately ambitious play. Trying to write it must have been rather like trying to build a cathedral—or a Golden City—single-handed. Wesker, like Andy, takes his inspiration from a cathedral. The play starts with a tape recording of Bach organ music and a rear projection of Durham Cathedral.

> ANDY (*with surprise*): I—am as big as—it. They built cathedrals for one man—it's just big enough. (*He

closes his eyes.) Show me love and I'll hate no one. Give me wings and I'll build you a city. Teach me to fly and I'll do beautiful deeds. (*He opens his eyes and looks up at the roof, turning round in wonderment at the same time.*) Hey God, do you hear that?

The action covers sixty-five years, and to succeed with it Wesker would have had to dramatize the process by which Andy's dream is partly realized, to make us believe in the struggle and in the City. With the struggle he partly succeeds. With the City he fails almost completely. We know more about Andy's rapture than about his plans. We know more about the opposition he encounters than we do about what the City is like. We believe readily enough in Andy's vision, but when we are told that the City has been built, we cannot altogether believe it because we cannot see it, even in our mind's eye.

Again, Wesker is talking about building Jerusalem in England's green and pleasant land. But this time he tries to fortify his rebels with a more realistic outlook, even at the beginning.

PAUL: But Andy's not even convinced himself. It's all patchwork, he says. How can he persuade others of a glory he doesn't believe in himself?

ANDY: If I decide to build those cities, then I'll forget they could ever have been regarded as patchwork, I'll ignore history.

PAUL: And what makes you think we'd ever agree to this massive piece of self-deception?

ANDY: Paul, if I'd come to you with brave declarations and the cry of an easy Utopia would you have believed that? (*Pause*)

PAUL: No, I'd not have believed that.

ANDY: Then what else is there left worth doing? The alternative was that complete revolution we all used to talk about, but there's no situation that's revolutionary, is there? Face it, all of you. There—is—no—revolutionary—situation.

> (*Andy challenges them all but there is only si-
> lence.*)
> Then let's begin.

"In other words" (to quote Wesker's own gloss on this passage of dialogue*) "they begin on a dream they know from the start is impossible and for this reason they reveal the picture of the state of the Left in Britain today. They do not live in a revolutionary situation, but must act. The result is doomed to compromise."

Certainly Wesker is more realistic than the fashionable rebels who do delude themselves that they are living in a revolutionary situation, but does the story of the play really reveal the state of the Left in Britain today? Certain key features are reproduced accurately enough: the power game played out by union leaders, the sterility of bureaucracy, the impossibility of cooperating with a group in the same way that the designers, artists, craftsmen and builders who constructed cathedrals cooperated with each other. But as a whole, the play does not succeed as well as the much more modest *Kitchen* in establishing itself as a valid image of British society.

Faced with the impossible task he had set himself, Wesker devised a variation on the ten-year gap method he used in *Chicken Soup with Barley*. The first of the two acts spans the years 1926–35. The first, last, and seventh of the twelve scenes in it are set in Durham Cathedral in 1926, when the young Andy, his girl friend Jessie, and his two friends Paul and Stoney are enthusing and planning for the future. Act Two begins in 1947, moves back (in its fourth scene) to 1926, forward (in its fifth and sixth) from 1948 to 1990, and back, at the end, to 1926.

In other words, the whole play is constructed out of a series of flash-forward scenes, using 1926 as the present and

* From the letter to Harold Ribalow.

setting the rest of the action in the future. Interesting though this idea is, it carries with it the disadvantages of ambiguity. Presented with a flashback, we know that the playwright un-equivocally wants us to believe that what we are watching has actually happened; presented with a series of flash-forwards, especially when some of them are set far ahead in the future, we cannot be entirely certain whether he is telling us that this is what will happen, or that this is what could happen, or that this is what the characters are imagining.

He also packs in so much political and personal material, moves so rapidly from one scene to the next, that the se-quence resembles a geometrical progression rather than the arithmetical progression we are used to. The first scene ends with Andy's forecast that he will qualify as an architect. In Scene Two (seven years later) we learn that he has done so. Scene Four ends with his issuing a challenging request to Jake Latham, the retiring chairman of a local trade union branch, which is rather like the challenging request Charles made to Pip in *Chips with Everything*—"Teach me." At the beginning of Scene Five, Jake is teaching him. Scene Eight (1935) ends with Andy's saying he does not want to go into local politics. Scene Nine (1936) starts when he is due back from a council meeting.

At first the rapid movement is exciting and satisfying, but we soon get the feeling that too much is being left out, too much is being taken up and dropped without being properly developed. Size and sweep alone do not make a cathedral: the detail of the parts needs to be worked out satisfactorily too. Above all we need a feeling of unity. The frustrations of this play often make us feel that it is not a single play we are watching: it is a compound of fragments of several different plays, some of which might have become extremely interest-ing had they been allowed to develop organically.

Brecht always took care to make each scene in his plays totally intelligible even to an audience unfamiliar with the politics and history of the period under discussion. An audience unfamiliar with the history of the British Labour Party would find it very hard to follow *Their Very Own and Golden City*. Many crucial points are made only in words, without being amplified in action, and Wesker makes the dangerous assumption that each line of dialogue spoken will register in the audience's mind. If it doesn't, they may easily get lost.

The play needs a much stronger backbone. Had it been developed, the relationship between Andy and Jake Latham could have provided one. The early confrontations between them are better written than anything else in the play. There are an economy and an incisiveness in the dialogue that produce an electric tension.

ANDY: I'm not afraid of a challenge.

JAKE: Challenge, is it? An optimist, are you?

ANDY: An optimist? Yes, brother, I suppose I am.

JAKE: Brother! Well, I mayn't ever have the opportunity to temper your optimism but I can advise you to drop the jargon. Brother! A useless title, full of empty love.

ANDY: A traditional greeting, Mr. Latham; it's got a good history.

JAKE: Use history, don't imitate it. Brother! Let's face facts! Let us stand together! It's only with strong determination that we can go forward! Jargon.

ANDY: If the old words are failing us then perhaps they'd better be rescued, not abandoned.

JAKE: Don't confuse breathing new life with the perpetuation of stale breath.

ANDY: You prefer homely maxims to jargon, is it?

JAKE: That was not a homely maxim and don't be cheeky.

ANDY: Don't be——?

JAKE: ——cheeky. I'm a clever man, Mr. Cobbam, but I'm an old and vain one. I could teach you a lot but I can't bear a young 'un who doesn't know his place.

ANDY: Know his——?

> JAKE: ——place. Stop gawping—you'll get lockjaw. I've
> no time for rebels, they hate the past for what it
> didn't give them. The Labour Movement is choked
> with bad-mannered, arrogant little rebels who enjoy
> kicking stubborn parents in the teeth. Revolutionaries
> is what we want—they spend less time rebelling
> against what's past and give their energy to the
> vision ahead.
>
> ANDY: "The vision ahead"? I thought that was the
> jargon we should drop, Mr. Latham.

After Andy has been shown *in statu pupillari* in relation to
Jake, it is dramatic when they clash at a public meeting in
1936 over the support that the Labour Party Conference had
voted to the League of Nations. Jake takes the line that was
taken, in reality, by the pacifist George Lansbury. As Wesker
points out in his letter to Ribalow, some of Jake's dialogue is
taken verbatim from Lansbury's speeches:

> Defeat doesn't matter. It the long run all defeat is
> temporary. It doesn't matter about present generations,
> but future ones always want to look back and know
> that someone was around acting on their beliefs, I can
> only tell you that I believe we were intended to live on
> this earth at peace with one another—if some people do
> not allow us to do this then I am ready to stand as the
> early Christians did and say—this is my faith, this is
> where I stand and if necessary, this is where I will die.

The audience responds enthusiastically, and Andy, whose
line of argument is based on the line Ernest Bevin took at the
1936 Party Conference, has a tough battle to win them over
to his side. He uses a phrase of Bevin's when he says:

> If you want Jake Latham to become a saint then let me
> make it easier for you by lighting the faggots for his
> martyrdom.

And he wins the day by virtue of his realism.

Facts:

In every fascist state it is the Labour movement that
has been attacked; who fondly thinks that in defeat it
will not happen here? The argument is for unity of
Labour's International Movement to prevent this war.
Facts:

Jake Latham is the man who calls for unity, but look—
he takes a stand that cracks the very solidarity he wants.
How dare he argue then for unity?

The argument is that in a war we should reply be para-
lysing every nation with a strike.
Facts:

Who will strike? The unions are destroyed in most of
Europe.

Who's left?

Confronted with these facts do we continue speaking
glibly about what could be achieved by strike in the
event of war? There only ever was one answer—the
international control of the seas and an economic pact
throughout the world which would control the sources
of our raw materials. That was an answer, at the time,
the right time. Now, it's too late. I'm sorry, Jake Latham,
saint, or no saint, it's too late. Those who can't accept
the movement's policy must take a course that is their
own—but not, I tell you, not inside this movement.

(*Applause, starting slowly, mounting to crescendo.*)

To say that the character of Jake is dropped in the second
half of the play would not be accurate. Andy refers to him by
name and, more dramatically, his influence is shown to survive in Andy's attitude. When Reginald Maitland, the Conservative Minister, warns Andy that if he goes on depending
on the T.U.C., the city will never be finished, Andy tellingly
echoes the sentiments we have heard voiced by Jake:

You see, Reggie, we've been at it for so long. I'd rather
see it in ruins than make that compromise. Ruins don't
matter, you can build on ruins, but future generations
always want to look back and know that someone was
around acting on principle. I want them to look back
and know about me. I know you want it finished, you're

a good man, but you mustn't ask me to make that compromise, not that one.

But the resounding question that Jake has posed is never
adequately answered by the play:

What holds a movement together? Any movement, not
even a movement, a group of people, say, or a family,
or a nation or a civilization? Something must. And *we*
didn't find it, God help us, *we* didn't find it.

And when Andy says that he owes most of his intellectual
development to Jake, it merely underlines the fact that this
has not sufficiently been substantiated by the one scene in
which we saw Jake "teaching" Andy. Wesker simply has not
given himself the space he needs.

Although it is interesting to see him threading political
history and personal relationships together in a new way, the
relationship with Jake is the only one that would have been
capable of development into the right kind of relevance to the
play's political themes. But Jake, unfortunately, has very little
to do with the building of the city. He belongs only to the
earlier phase of Andy's career.

In the later phase, the personal and political elements tend
to separate. As Ronald Bryden said in his review, there is a
hint that Wesker sees Andy's failure as linked in some way to
the failure of his marriage.* As far as I can make out, the
linkage is a very loose one, hinging on Wesker's view that a
good marriage is integral to a good life, and the good life of
the sort Andy dreams about turns out to be unattainable. In
any case, the marriage is given only summary treatment,
though there are some very moving moments in which Jessie
protests at Andy's way of treating her as a mere housekeeper.
It is only with Kate that he opens out in conversation. Though

* As Wesker sees it, the connection between a failure of love and
a failure in the world outside is a basic and vital theme not only in
this play but in the trilogy and in *The Four Seasons.*

there is no serious dramatic attempt to connect this betrayal of Jessie with the betrayal of his original dream in the compromise he makes with Maitland, the parallel is there to be inferred.

The central relationship, in so far as there is one, is with Kate. In their early scenes, there is some good, hard-hitting dialogue:

> There are certain people who are born with natures that naturally deserve love and respect. Yours, like mine, is one of them.
>
> ANDY: I think you're seeing me as you want.
>
> KATE: Oh? You really see yourself as a humble man? *You* shame yourself with false modesty?
>
> ANDY: I don't see how modesty is always false, any more than knowing I'm capable and ambitious means I'm immodest. I am what I am, I don't feel the need to boast it loudly or deny it. What I do is my boast, not what I say or don't say.
>
> KATE: Charming, Andy, it becomes you.
>
> ANDY: And I'm not needing your comments.
>
> KATE: Don't be ungracious.
>
> ANDY: I'm annoyed.
>
> KATE: Don't get annoyed either, it's my nature to be direct.
>
> ANDY: It's your nature to be a lot of things, it seems. Do you always talk about yourself?
>
> KATE: I want us to be friends.
>
> ANDY: You want, you want! You'll have to earn, young lady.
>
> KATE: How long have you lived here?
>
> ANDY: Eighteen months.
>
> KATE (*referring to a chair*): Did you buy that monstrosity or does it belong here?
>
> ANDY: It belongs here.
>
> KATE: Why don't you get rid of it?
>
> ANDY: It belongs here.
>
> KATE: My dear, the landlady should be given to understand that you are doing her a kindness by getting rid of it.

ANDY: It's not my habit to interfere with other people's property.

KATE: And you're the socialist, are you? Look at this room. You want to be an architect? You want to build beautiful homes? Then how can you surround yourself with ugliness? Look how you dress, look what you hang on your walls. How can you dare plan other people's houses when you live with such mediocrity?

ANDY: I——

KATE: How can you dare?

ANDY: I—blast you, woman, I'll not have anyone talk at me like this.

KATE: Honesty hurts you, then?

ANDY: It's your tone of voice, it gets in the way.

But just as there is no clear focus on the way Andy's speech patterns develop from these to those of Sir Andrew Cobham at the end of the play, so there is no clear focus on the development of the relationship itself. Towards the end, Kate is just used as an extra voice in dialogues requiring one. Wesker has told me in conversation that he thought it was clear that there was no sexual relationship between Kate and Andrew. It was not clear to me, and I have since found another critic (Ronald Bryden) who was puzzled on the same point.

Another sign of failure in the montage of scenes is that some of them (like Jessie's onslaught in Act Two, Scene Six) have a sharper impact than others. Aspects of personal life seem altogether too arbitrarily chosen for detailed treatment. The breakdown of Andy's health is telescoped too much for it to have any great dramatic effect, and there is even a hint of special pleading in the way it is linked to the way that the unions have let him down.

This too is dehydrated rather than dramatized. Given a chance of owning the means of production, the unions decide not to take it. But we do not see how the decision is reached. It is presented to us as a *fait accompli*:

ANDY: What's been decided?
WORTHINGTON: Not all you hoped for, Andy.
ANDY: What's been decided?
CAMBRIDGE: You don't really expect them to vote in industry, you didn't really, did you? Private enterprise, let them do it, it's their job, not ours Andy lad. Believe me, our own fights are enough. He didn't really hope for it, Ted.

This is much more crucial to the action than the decision which was treated at such length in Part One—and at local level—about what attitude was to be adopted toward rearmament. The reason it was treated at such length was that it provided an arena for the conflict between Andy and Jake. The real failure of the play is a failure of conception. The central image (the cathedral), the main relationships (with Jake and with Kate), and the main themes (the attempt at creating a new Socialist Society *in parvo* and the necessity of compromise with the Establishment) are all pulling the play in different directions. There can be no way of treating and developing all these elements at the same time.

Had the play been developing in the right way—as a unity —a scene like Andy's soliloquy after the banquet would have attained an almost Lear-like resonance and pathos. Nothing less could be adequate to fill out the cathedral-like dimensions Wesker aspires to. But the actual level of the writing here is lower than in *Chips with Everything* and lower than it was in the early scenes with Jake and with Kate.

ANDY: I must stop clenching my teeth, I really must try and prevent my teeth from clenching. Howl, that's what I'd do if I opened my mouth—howl. Unclench your teeth, you old fool you. But why is it that I don't want to talk? Because I don't, you know, not a word. One day—I know it—one day I shan't even see people and then what'll happen. I shall stay just still like, petrified, because I won't be able to find a single reason why I should make one word follow another, one thought follow another.

There, look, my teeth were clenched again.

Do you know what depresses me? Men need leaders, that's what depresses me. They'll wait another twenty years and then another leader will come along and they'll build another city. That's all. Patchwork! Bits and pieces of patchwork. Six cities, twelve cities, what difference. Oases in the desert, that the sun dries up. Jake Latham, Jake Latham—ah, Jake Latham.

My lifelong boys! *My* lifelong boys? Prefects! That's all; the Labour movement provides prefects to guard other men's principles for living. Oh we negotiate for their better application, shorter working week and all that but—prefects! They need them, we supply them.

Still, nothing wrong in that I suppose; a bargain! A gentlemen's agreement, understood by everybody. They let us build the old Golden City or two, even help us and in the end—look at me! I don't suppose there's such a thing as democracy, really, only a democratic way of manipulating power. And equality? None of that either, only a gracious way of accepting inequality.

(*Jessie enters, carrying a card tables and a pack of cards. Kate, Harrington and Maitland also appear. They have come for a game of bridge.*)

Look again, they were clenched again. Unclench them. Silly old fool, you. Unclench them.

You shouldn't force people to dirty themselves. A man loves the world only when he loves himself, and what love do you have left for yourself, Andrew Cobham?

This is depressingly like a mixture of *King Lear, Endgame* and an average television script. And at the end of the play we get another embarrassing game:

ANDY: Right, my ragged-arsed brothers—mount your horses.

(*Two of the boys link arms behind. The third grips their arms and bends down. Jessie climbs on to his back and is now riding a "chariot."*)

We knew the door was open.

JESSIE: How did you know, my ragged-arsed brothers?

ANDY: Because we're on the side of the angels, lass.

JESSIE: —and are people good?

ANDY: Aye—and people are good.

JESSIE (*whipping them*): Giddy up, stallions. Forward, you ragged-arsed brothers—forward!

> (*The "chariot" gallops off.*
> *Moonlight strikes through the coloured glass.*
> *Silence.*)

The Four Seasons

Though premièred before *Their Very Own and Golden City*, *The Four Seasons* was written after it. It is not a success, but it is not a complete and uninteresting failure, as reviews of the London production suggest. It is the only play by Wesker which can be described—in so far as any play can be described—as totally unpolitical. It is a play about love in which there are no other characters than the two lovers. There is no plot and only the simplest pattern of development: the relationship, like the year which the lovers spend together, passes through four seasonal stages. Emotional hibernation is followed by the budding of a love which ripens in the summer and goes to seed in the winter. But there will be no repetition of the cycle for these lovers. At least not with each other.

Explanations are whittled down to a minimum. We never find out who the house belongs to, why it is left empty for a year, or how Adam and Beatrice manage about food and electricity and a water supply. Or how they met or how they came to agree to spend a year together. So far as possible, they are abstracted from any social context. We hear a certain amount about their previous relationships—they have both had a marriage and at least one infidelity—but during the year, they have relationships with no one except each other. Time is telescoped and language is heightened. Sometimes successfully, often not. Wesker is also confronted with the problem of how to present the development of the relationship through dramatic action and not through words eked out by theatrical activity. Here too success is intermittent.

Suspense is successfully sustained throughout the first season by the device of keeping Beatrice silent. So far as the audience knows, she might start answering at any minute.

> Say "eyes" or "lips," say. Or point. Do that, even. Just point. Not even that?
> Listen to the wood crackling. Smell it?
>> (*She breathes in, slowly, slightly.*)
> Again, Beatrice, again.
>> (*Again she breathes in, this time a deeper breath.*)
> Again, can you do it again?
>> (*She turns her head away; for his foolish persistence she has, for the moment dismissed him. He can understand nothing.*)
> You think I don't understand, don't you? How I recognize that look. The female dismissing the male.

Sometimes, however, Adam settles down into what is all too clearly a monologue:

> And yet I know. Why should I mock you? I know. I've also loved and been loved. But I destroyed that love. Why should I mock you?
> You were right to dismiss me, we don't really know each other. Even though I look at you and see myself and try to guess yet—I don't know. Poor girl, we grieve for ourselves don't we?

Or into narrative which is mannered and self-intoxicated:

> But she had her glory, my wife, her retribution. One day a young man came from another country to be our

guest. He had eyes like an uncertain child in a strange and festive room and he laughed with deep pleasure at everything he saw. You could show him nothing and take him nowhere that didn't offer him delight. And gradually I saw my wife unfold from her misery as she gathered her heart and her senses to carry him from one place to another. All the secret corners of our own past she revealed to him and he held her hand and blessed her kindness as they walked over bridges and looked into the river and ate in friendly restaurants—the tested gestures of love.

The passage of time from winter to spring is marked by a pause in which both of them appear to be sleeping. Then, as a long ray of sunshine cuts into the room, Beatrice wakes, goes out to pick bluebells and decorates the sleeping Adam from head to foot. Their opening dialogue is less certain of itself than the gesture:

ADAM: I've not had such a beautiful thing done to me since——

BEATRICE: See what we give to the people we comfort? The tested gestures of love.

ADAM: You garlanded your lover with bluebells?

BEATRICE: Every morning.

ADAM: And at night?

BEATRICE: I oiled my skin with a different scent.

ADAM: You worshipped him?

BEATRICE: What else do you do to the man you love?

ADAM: Some women make their lovers wait and offer love as though it were a favour.

BEATRICE: Your sluts and your whores do that, but not your women, not your real women.

ADAM: Then you're a rare woman. Now what is it? Your face has fallen again.

BEATRICE: So many people have once considered me a rare woman.

ADAM: But aren't you? You seem so sure, so confident, even your silence was so confident. Look at you. Soft skin, proud cheeks, penetrating eyes—one knows. Too penetrating, perhaps, too intelligent—but sad also, and such weariness, such haunting, worldly weariness. One knows.

Altogether, the problem of poetic language remains unsolved. In an "epilogue" he has written to the play, Wesker himself gives an example of the difficulties he had:

In the rehearsal script of the play and throughout the production Adam told Beatrice that she had "autumn soft skin." For me this conjured up the image of walks through the wind and soft colours of autumn landscapes —until someone insisted the image belonged more to a television advert for Camay Soap. I resisted the suggestion at first but finally acknowledged it and deleted the words.

But there are many other phrases which without belly-flopping quite so badly into cliché fail to dive deep enough into their subject.

There is also some confusion of purpose and some arbitrariness in the treatment of the relationship. Wesker's aim, as he says, was to provide enough information to ensure that the audience could concentrate wholly on the relationship:

A major problem then: what kind of information? That which seemed inevitable. For instance, neither Adam nor Beatrice mentions to whom the house belongs. Adam could have said that it belonged to his father but such information is timid; it would have jarred and made no difference to their subsequent relationship.

But in adducing facts from the past which do make a difference to it, he is haphazard in his selection and liable to be swept off his course by an uncertain and half-hearted lyricism. This tempts him into prolonging certain narratives beyond their merits. Beatrice's, for instance, about her lover:

There was nothing he or I could touch either that didn't explode.

What battles we fought. I thought I saw God in him but we fought. The boy with wings. I used to sit at his feet, literally, curled on the floor, hugging him, "Get up," he'd say, he hated it, "get up, off your knees, no woman should be on her knees to a man." He never believed he was worth such devotion, it embarrassed him.

And I was dead, a piece of nothing until he touched me, or spoke to me, or looked at me. Even his look was an embrace. I used to nag him for all his thoughts, hungry for everything that passed through his mind, jealous that he might be thinking of something he couldn't share with me. And sometimes he'd be thinking of nothing and he'd say, "Blank! My mind's a blank; must silence always signify profound thoughts, silly woman?" And I'd tell him I didn't care, I still couldn't take my eyes off him. His face was made of love, despite himself, and I knew every curve and movement his features made; I don't know why we fought.

That's a lie. I knew very well why we fought. I couldn't bear to see the shadow of another person fall on him. Even hearing him talk to someone else on the phone was enough to make prickles of the hair on my neck. How dared he think my intellect was not enough to set to right his silly world's intolerable pain! Do you know what I used to do? Oh we're awful creatures all right; sneer. I used to sneer and denigrate anyone who was near and dear to him—friends, relatives, colleagues. Even his children, lovely, large, innocent infants, even them, I couldn't bear the demands they made on him. When they were desperately ill I dismissed their complaints as childish maladies, and when they cried because their father constantly stayed away I accused them of artfulness. No one missed the whip of my sneers.

But he was a leader of men and leaders of men fight back. Every word became a sword, every sword a giant bomb destroying nerve centers, crippling the heart. We hurled anything at each other: truths, lies, half-truths—what did it matter, as long as it was poison, as long as we gave each other no peace. Sometimes he would give in, for love of me, and when the next battle came round I would taunt him with his previous surrender; and when he didn't surrender I would accuse him of being afraid of his wife. No peace, none at all, neither for him or myself.

Adam's monologues are better written than this, on the whole, and we form from them a clearer picture of him than we ever form of her. But they often suffer from the same wordiness and the same confusion of purpose, being neither specific enough to pull their weight as contributions to the characterization nor poetic enough to lift the level of communication off the prosaic ground.

This, I think, is part of what Martin Esslin meant when he called the play* "expressionistic in form, neo-romantic in content." Adam's and Beatrice's narratives tell part of the story of how they both came to be in the emotional state that they are in but the construction is a long way removed from naturalism (though I wouldn't, myself, have labelled it *expressionist*.) As an example of "neo-romanticism," Martin Esslin cites Maeterlinck who was "delighted in the *atmosphere* of naturalism while disliking the prosaic quality of much of the detail. So he went for atmosphere plus highly poetic language." Maeterlinck's language is very wishy-washy; Wesker's instinct is always to be objective. But whereas, in his best plays, *The Kitchen* and *Chips with Everything*, his instinct towards objectivity works hand-in-hand with a confidence about what to select, in *The Four Seasons* he has been unable to hammer out for himself any principle to guide his selection.

The parts of the play in which he comes nearest to finding firm ground are the parts in which Adam and Beatrice relate to each other through an activity like singing or cooking an

---

* In *Plays and Players*, November 1965.

apple strudel. Both the singing lesson and the cooking chart their progress through a definite phase of their relationship and if Wesker had tried to delineate the whole development of their love in terms like these, he would have stood a chance, at least, of succeeding.

With only two characters and a predictable pattern of progress, the play could hold the audience's interest only through a series of constant surprises over the way in which things happen. Far too often, nothing is happening at all. This is not merely a matter of whether Wesker is working through words or through actions. When Beatrice pulls Adam gently round the room, admiring him from different angles, something is happening which is carrying the story of their affair one step further. When they quarrel there is a similar suspense and a similar development. Interaction is in progress. But when either of them embark on long narratives or rhapsodies, all the other can do is listen, and we become aware that the action is being suspended for the sake of verbal flourishes which aim consciously at the "poetic."

> You know, when I was born I was born with a great laughter in me. Can you believe that? A great laughter, like a blessing. And some people loved and some hated it. It was a sort of challenge, a test against which people measured themselves as human beings; and I could never understand, not at all, the desperateness of either their love or their hatred. Have you ever been with a beautiful woman, a really breathtaking beauty, and watched or felt the passionate waves of devotion and loathing that she attracts, and noticed how the people around feel the irresistible need to say sly, unpleasant things to show they're not intimidated by her beauty? So it was with my laughter.
>
> And she, who had no need to measure herself against anything or anyone because she was so endowed with her own loveliness, her own intelligence—she too began to measure herself against that laughter. And why? Because it belonged to me you see; I was *born* with it, she

couldn't bear that it had not been bestowed by her and so she began to measure herself against me and challenge all that was mine.

She found enemies where there were none and saw betrayals in every act. She broke each smile and stormed every moment of peace we had built. And once, when I wrote to her from a sick bed and cursed her, when I lost control, she suddenly became calm and took control as if to show that in fact she had bestowed that laughter on me, and only she could nurse me back to health. "That laughter is our child," she said. "Now, at last, only I can look after it. You," she said, "are incapable."

The time that is saved by not explaining the circumstances of the action is wasted by letting the characters explain themselves to each other in words instead of demonstrating themselves in action. It is true that Beatrice is later to react against the way he uses her for this kind of confidence, but by then it merely produces the effect of going back to pick up a stitch which has been dropped. The opportunity of sustaining constant interaction has been wasted.

There is also more bad writing in this play than in any other of Wesker's.

BEATRICE: I have a golden eagle for a lover.

ADAM: But the sun has burnt his wings.

BEATRICE: Nothing shall burn your wings—I am your sun.

ADAM: Where shall I fly?

BEATRICE: Anywhere—as long as you carry me with you.

ADAM: But you're my sun.

BEATRICE: When you need me to be your sun, I'm your sun. When you need soft winds I shall cover the land with my breath. When you need comfort then I shall offer my breasts and my limbs and my lips. Whatever you call for you shall have.

ADAM: And you? What shall I give you?

BEATRICE: Every second. Every touch, every thought, every feeling. Every second you shall give me.

Another weakness is that the essential element of physicality is almost completely missing from this love relationship. If the poetry were better it might provide a substitute for it, but as it is, such references as there are to love-making only make us feel that the whole picture of their love-making, discovering each other and then losing each other is falsified by leaving sex out of it. What we need is a kind of stylization which makes the whole question irrelevant. There are passages which make gestures in the direction of establishing the right convention, but moments like the one when Adam slaps Beatrice's face violate the half-formed convention of nonphysicality.

Towards the end of the play, the writing suddenly reaches a much higher level. Wesker seems to be arriving at a theatrical rhetoric not unlike John Whiting's in his earlier plays like *A Penny for a Song*:

> BEATRICE: What do I remember?
> A long drive into the autumn countryside I remember. The astonishment we shared that trees and fields could burn with such colours. The tremendous blaze of dying hedges, the smouldering leaves, the discovery of these things.
> I remember the plots against indifference, the ease with which we picked up each other's thoughts in our battles with the world, the language we gave each other. I remember the long walks into the long nights, the gratitude for his presence, my helplessness.
> And I remember that when my father died in a far-off country I did not go to his side because I wanted to stay with *him*. And my father died alone —I was his favourite child. These things I remember. And you? Tell me the beautiful things you remember about her.
> ADAM: Moments of music and silence and adoration I remember. The attention of her eyes. I remember the devotion of her limbs and the care she gave to everything she did for me from the tender binding of a

present to the intimate cooking of a meal. I remember my cruelty and I remember her cruelty. These things.

I remember that we were not afraid to dance when we couldn't, to say we did not know things we should have known or admit each unimportant sin we had committed against each other. I remember that we were not afraid to laugh hysterically or to play with children or to grow old. I remember we were not afraid.

I remember my father dying and my holding his head in my hands and crying, "Keep breathing, come on, don't give up Joe, don't stop Joe." And my mother, through her tears, saying, "You think he'll listen to you," and smiling, and both of us sobbing and me wanting to run my hands continually over his eyes and cheeks and hair. These things I remember. Because moments like these remind me that time passes and time passing reminds me of sadness and waste and neglect and suffering. And I know in my heart that all those lovely moments of youth will not return. These things I remember, and because of it I'm a gentler person, it is easier for me to forgive and be forgiven. These things, Beatrice, these things I remember and know, just as you know and, for that reason, you will be gentler.

In this last passage, Adam and Beatrice are not merely talking about memories of their lovers, they are also talking about the memories they will retain of each other—an irony which makes the whole sequence dramatic. Admittedly, it is not altogether digested into its context and the play ends abruptly after it with a brief scene of action as Adam tries to light a fire with an armful of dry leaves and as Beatrice methodically packs. But we have had a tantalizing glimpse of a totally different Wesker.

The Friends

There are probably more productions than most people realize in which the rehearsal conflicts between director and actors—if only they could be recorded—would prove to be more interesting and dramatic than the dialogue of the play. *The Friends* is an example.

Determined to direct it himself, Wesker turned down an opportunity to have it staged at the Royal Court by another director; instead he accepted an invitation to have it premiered in Stockholm in his own production. Five months later Eddie Kulukundis, a shipowner making his first independent venture into theatrical management, gave him a chance to direct it in England. They collected a very good cast and Wesker invited the actors to his farmhouse in Wales for a week's holiday combined with read-throughs and discussions. In that week and the subsequent rehearsal period he antagonized them to the point where they were no longer willing to take direction from him or even to let him talk to them.

The script is static and lacking in theatrical liveliness. It soon became obvious that the cast was losing faith in him as a leader who could help them animate it. From Wesker's point of view the actors were all limited by the conditioning

and the insecurity they had acquired in the conventional theater; from their point of view he was too inexperienced as a
director and too uncritical of himself as a writer even to
understand their problems in trying to keep the waterlogged
text afloat. The unhappiness and the personal hostilities that
developed must have affected the resultant performance,
which was plodding and unshaped—anything but redolent of
the close intimacy between the "friends" that the action demands. But no director would have been able to make it into
a good play, unless he could have persuaded Wesker to re-
write it.

The basic idea is an interesting one. Like the Beatles, the
friends are of North-country and working-class origin, and
they have been phenomenally successful while still very
young. Now they are facing middle age, and one of them is
dying. Like Albee's *All Over*, *The Friends* depends heavily on
the drama of approaching death: almost nothing happens in
either play except that a pivotal character dies. In both plays
the death releases floods of loquacious self-revelation from all
the other characters—and in *The Friends* from the dying girl
herself. The enforced realization that their youth is over pre-
cipitates a crisis of self-knowledge and self-disgust in the others.

The friends are designers, and their manager, Macey, calls
them "six of the most talented people in the field." This is a
valuation Wesker clearly wants us to accept, but there is
nothing in the play to persuade us. His idea of the work they
have done as designers is as vague and undeveloped as his
idea of the architect's part in designing the cities of *Their
Very Own and Golden City*. The friends are meant to have
painted and designed for large architectural projects and to
own a chain of shops which sell articles manufactured to
their designs, but the humorless soul-searchings Wesker
writes for them suggests a stolidity and dullness which would
hardly be compatible with the talent necessary to produce
designs that would catch the public fancy. Brisk bright dia-

logue such as Alun Owen wrote for the Beatles' films would have served the play's purposes better.

There are six friends. Five of them were at art college together in Leeds: Manfred, his sister Esther, her boyfriend Roland, Crispin and his girl friend Tessa. The sixth, Simone, is a girl from an upper-class family who joined the group later. The only other character in the play is Macey, the manager, who is Jewish. Whether any of the others are meant to be Jewish is not clear, though their language sometimes suggests it.

The dialogue opens in a vein reminiscent of Virginia Woolf's *The Waves*, but Wesker handles the technique more crudely:

> ROLAND: Last night I slept very soundly. Long and deep.
> MANFRED: (*reading*) "The electron is a completely universal fundamental particle . . ."
> ROLAND: I can't remember the last time I slept so soundly.
> MANFRED: ". . . It is stable and long-lived. For all practical purposes it is indestructible and is at present in the universe in inexhaustible numbers . . ."
> ESTHER: And Baroque churches and houses, fountains and market-places and the music of organs and Norman arches and wine and the cooking of friends and the sound of friends.

Without giving us any reason to be interested in these characters Wesker exposes us to the sub-poetry of their free-associating, expecting us to be immediately caught up in their emotional lives. Their self-absorption soon becomes tiresome and the writing becomes the naive accomplice of their self-importance:

> MANFRED: Who do I hate, who do I love; what do I value, what do I despise; what pleases, what offends me? Them's thoughts, them is.

> ROLAND: And I shall cease to be obese. It's so humili-
> ating to have a body that won't do what you want it
> to do. I would stop using words if I could.
> CRISPIN: Do you know I've stopped reading in the
> lavatory. I kept feeling it was an insult to the writer.

Since Wesker fails to involve the audience in the friends'
inner lives, it is inevitable that the climaxes—like the moment
when Manfred denies the existence of evil—have very little
effect.

As in *Their Very Own and Golden City*, the aim is to
construct a perspective of disillusionment in which the characters see their earlier idealism in a colder, more realistic
light. But their past aspirations and successes do not become
any more real or compelling for us than their present depression. So much of the play depends on statements they make
about themselves, rather than on dramatization, that even the
attempts to differentiate the three boys from one another are
only partially successful. The differentiation between the
three girls is more effective because more physical, less de-
pendent on words. But none of the relationships between them
spark into three-dimensional life. Though occasionally there
are theatrically effective moments—as when Crispin venge-
fully embarrasses Simone by reading to the others the love
letters she has written to him—for the most part the characters make statements rather than demonstrations. Simone's
explanation of the sympathy she feels towards the working
classes, Macey's long speech about not loving his wife, and
Manfred's apologia about the poverty of all their intentions,
are expository and undramatic—tangents to a circle which
has nothing at its center except Wesker's own conscience and
consciousness.

Most of the writing in the play would have come nearer to
passing muster if it had been in diary form. The reflections on
the amount of suffering there is in the world, for instance,
sound like a half-heartedly dramatized journal. Macey's ac-

count of his attitude to the young is only interesting in so far as it bears on Wesker's attitude to the young, while Esther's attempt at an analysis of the differences between the rebel and the revolutionary are not interesting at all.

Some of the emotionality in the play has the ring of Victorian melodrama:

> Look how she sleeps; so sweet. What the hell do I care for the dead knowledge of evil when I'm blessed with a sister as sweet as this?

Roland's burning of three pound notes is an innocent repetition of a theatrical cliché, and Crispin's confession that he goes to bed with old ladies is all the more embarrassing for being totally unconvincing. Much of his dialogue is written in broad North-country dialect and he explains that he is talking that way "so's not to see the seriousness of it." The macabre ending in which the friends play games with Esther's dead body makes an uncomfortable theatrical impact without resolving anything, and Roland's appearance in a blood-soaked shirt is another desperate bid at theatricality. We are told that he has been cutting his body with a razor and rubbing salt into the wounds because his girl friend is dying:

> Please God make it hurt more. I've never had any pain in my life, make it hurt more, it's not fair to give pain so unevenly, make it, make it.

Altogether *The Friends* is such a bad play that it becomes very hard to remember how well Wesker has sometimes written.

The Old Ones

The Old Ones is a lot less static than *The Friends*, and because it flashes fairly briskly from one locale to another, the play seems a lot less static than it is. We have twenty-five fairly short scenes divided among seven different settings, and the movement from one place, one group of characters, one rhythm, to another greatly reduces the dangers of monotony.

But the play has a lot in common with *The Friends*, sharing not only its preoccupation with aging and the approach of death but its method. The friends were all between thirty-five and thirty-eight, and it was Esther's leukemia that made death a reality for them; in *The Old Ones* seven of the ten important characters are between about sixty-eight and about seventy-two. No one dies, but even the characters who are not so close to death are very aware of it. Talking to her seventy-one-year-old mother, Rosa, who is thirty-two, says that the most terrible fact she knows is that one day she will die; she grieves as much over the prospect of her own death as over that of her mother's. Rosa quotes Boswell's question, "But is not the fear of death natural to man?" and Johnson's answer, "So much so, sir, that the whole of life is but keeping away the thoughts of it." And she goes on to promise that she will not die happily with a sweet smile: she will rage. Wesker is echoing the Dylan Thomas lines he quotes as epigraph from the play:

> Do not go gentle into that good night,
> Old age should burn and rave at close of day;
> Rage, rage against the dying of the light.

His other epigraph is from Carlyle:

> Frightful to all men is death, from of old called King of Terrors.

In an article for *The Listener* (18 May 1972) Ronald Bryden, play adviser for the Royal Shakespeare Company, said that the kind of play he was looking for had "a solid, three-dimensional interplay of identities, each real as the other, in which each question has a multiplicity of answers and each situation can be changed without anyone having to walk out of the imprisoning doll's house, like Ibsen's Nora. I'd call that a real image of society, able to speak of all its classes." This, one feels, is the kind of play Wesker was trying to write in *The Old Ones*.

The seventy-year-old twin brothers, Emanuel and Boomy, are seen in conflict with each other, though the fighting is mainly verbal and the conflict mainly one of attitudes. Boomy is characterized as a prophet of doom, much under the spell of Carlyle, while Emanuel, despite bouts of neurasthenic gloominess, is presented mainly as an advocate of joy. Boomy is also seen in conflict with his son, Martin, who is twenty-eight, and Emanuel is shown in conflict with his lame wife, Gerda, whose attitudes are more commonsensical than his. But though the play as a whole is less didactic than *The Friends*, it cannot be said that all the characters are equally solid, or that there is real interplay between them, or that each question is allowed to have a multiplicity of answers.

If *The Old Ones* too often comes too close to being a

direct statement, it is a statement not so much about what life is like for the very old as about the possibility and the necessity of joy. Some of the best moments in Wesker's previous plays have been outbreaks of joy, either private—as with Beatie in *Roots* in her two explosions, one into dance, and the other into speech—or corporate, as in *Chips with Everything*, when the rhythm of the old peasant revolt song "The Cutty Wren" gradually gets a hold on the recruits, and they all join in. In *The Old Ones* the whole play is subject to a strong gravitational pull towards the Hasidic joy.

Hasidism was a mystical development of Judaism which began in 18th-century Poland. It stressed the immanence of God, urging that he be served through joy. It strongly influenced Martin Buber, who is quoted several times in *The Old Ones*. The play also contains quotations from the Baal Shem-Tov, the founder of Hasidism: "He who is full of joy, is full of love for men and all fellow creatures."

Although there are Jewish characters and backgrounds in the majority of Wesker's previous plays, he had never before made any extended use of the religious rituals. Religious rituals always have great theatrical potential; in addition, it is always fascinating to watch something being constructed on stage—a fact David Storey exploited in *The Contractor*. *The Old Ones* starts by tapping both these resources: we see some of the characters constructing a Succah, the ritual tabernacle used in the Festival of Tabernacles, otherwise known, as we are told in the opening speech, as "the season of our joy." Later, branches and leaves are brought in to decorate the Succah, and this part of the play is worked to a climax when, following instructions out of a book (as if none of them would otherwise know what to do), the characters, moving branches in the air, enact a variant on the procession which is normally part of the synagogue service during the festival. Then they become self-conscious, put the branches away, and sit down to eat.

Sarah, the seventy-one-year-old sister of Emanuel and

Boomy, is essentially the same character as Sarah Kahn in the trilogy, though now older, and modeled equally closely on the playwright's mother. In fact, Wesker recorded a lot of his mother's conversation when he started working on the play; much of it was incorporated in the dialogue and helped build a three-dimensional and amusing character. Her defense of the working class is delightful:

> Look! (*Picks up a letter.*) A letter from my brother in Roumania. Someone had to bring it to my door, how do you think it got here? Carrier pigeon? You're making tea, you've got milk, every morning there's a pint of milk at my door. Who brings it? Prince Philip? And who do you think got it from the cow? His wife? Look (*switches light on and off*). Light? How did it get here? (*Moves to the telephone.*) You want to speak to your sister in America? Speak! Turn this, wait a little, a voice answers. Who's putting you through? Who does it? Everywhere you look—new buildings, new roads, new cities—who puts them there? So leave me alone about my working class. (*Continues baking.*)

But a lot of the dialogue used to characterize the others is heavy handed, especially when it lapses, as it often does, into monologue. Teressa, who is about sixty-eight, is given three solo scenes, two in Act One, one in Act Two, before she is brought into an ensemble scene. She is lonely, with lumbago, a weak bladder, coughing fits, a pain behind her ears, and a pain in her chest. She soliloquizes and works spasmodically at translating poetry, reading out alternative renderings of a passage she has trouble with. To make a character like this sympathetic and interesting when presented through monologues, the writing would have to be extraordinary. Her monologues tend to dwell rather too explicitly on her suffering and her preoccupations:

> Ach! Books! Thoughts! If they live in your head and you can't use them—useless! Mocking! Fifteen years I've been translating you, Wanda my darling. (*Moves again to*

mirror.) Look at my face. When did you last see a face that said *so* much. It's all there, Teressa, full of lines. Disappointment, bitterness, self-hatred, surprise, fear. Sour—all sour, my darling.

(*She turns away unhappily; then looks back again, defiantly.*)

I want to look beautiful!

(*Shrugs. Moves to cut a slice of bread, butters it and eats it with a lump of cheese, indifferently.*)

(*Full mouth.*) Silly woman! Silly, silly woman, Teressa. (*Pause.*) What's silly about wanting to look beautiful again? Vanity? It's vain to want to look in the mirror and get pleasure? I tell you, with that kind of pleasure I'd be so generous, so generous and calm and dignified. Sweetness, darling, there's such a sweetness in beauty. Oh dear. Oh dear, dear me. (*Pushes away food.*) Who can eat?

Not only are there too many monologues in the play but the dialogue generally tends towards the condition of monologue—and there is too much direct self-explication. The point that the old people are leading aimless, lonely, bored lives is made through their own statements of their awareness of these things. In his depressive phases, Emanuel speaks to his wife very much as if he were speaking to himself. Rudi, Sarah's nephew, a painter, speaks as if he is carrying on a nonstop conversation with himself:

I go on because I know if you don't go on for yourself you've had it; with jealousy from this one from that one, you wouldn't believe people can be so jealous, in every place, over everything, one person watching you, another one frightened in case you get more marks than them, you know what I mean? Like this I paint and I keep track where the paintings go. No one lets their work go somewhere without them knowing; you can be swindled. But me? I got photographs, with my name, on both sides, and it's proof and one day they'll sell and I'll earn money enough to take no notice of the lot of them. And they want me, you know that? To give my paintings. They chase me, write to me, the librarian, to bring, to hang. Because people, you know, they don't like reality, they hate reality, they're frightened. That's why there's all these goings on with revolutions and riots and violence. But it costs money—for paints, for hardboard, for framing.

The less dramatic give-and-take there is in the dialogue, the less convincing Wesker seems to be able to make it. The least credible character of all is Jack, the only old man in the play who is not Jewish. A neighbor of Sarah's, he behaves as if he were mad, shouting out warnings in the street, and ringing a bell, like a leprous and demented town crier.

Don't come you near me, don't come you near me, the plague is upon me, the devil is in me.

We are told that he is not insane and we are intended, I think, to infer that he has invented his own madness as a diversion from loneliness, boredom and self-hatred. When he is explaining himself to Sarah, he tells how despicable his past behavior has been.

Basically the conception of Jack is a sentimental one. He builds up a picture of himself as a man who refused water to a dying fellow soldier, but towards the end of Act One he is offering help to Sarah's friend Millie:

Hated the army, hated the war, hated employers and all their sweet smiles; and I learned that a man's got ter give 'is warning and cry stinking fish sometimes. But—I loves London and I loves England and I loves the little foreigners like you wot they let in to mix the blood a bit. Come, missus, me arm, I'll escort you safe and sound to the other little Jewish lady wots my neighbour. (*She takes his arm, shyly.*) And wot a neighbour she is, she is. A fighter, a real little pellet of steel she is. Pellets of steel all you lot are. Come.

Rosa, Sarah's daughter, works as a careers advisory officer for the Ministry of Education, and her lectures to high-school seniors are also monologues.

> Nor is it only a matter of what *you're* suited for, is it? But what suits you. After all, I think insufficient attention is paid to what is likely to make us feel fulfilled. Society isn't very good at that yet, is it?

There are two monologues in which recorded noises and projections of jeering faces tell us that she is not going down at all well with the schoolchildren. Then, after a heart-to-heart talk with Sarah, she finds herself suddenly able to dominate her unruly audience.

Besides monologue, there is an excessive amount of quotation in the play. With their rival attitudes to life, the twin brothers communicate largely by banging on the wall that separates their rooms and thundering quotations at each other—Carlyle, Voltaire, Ecclesiastes, and Buber. This exchange leads, not ineffectively, to the play's climax, in which Emanuel seems to be quoting but is in fact speaking his own words. This is reminiscent of the climax in *Roots* when Beatie finds she is no longer voicing Ronnie's thoughts but her own.

Some of the confrontations between Martin and his parents are also reminiscent of the trilogy—of Ronnie in *Chicken Soup with Barley* and *I'm Talking about Jerusalem*. Wesker does well to restrain himself from developing the melodrama inherent in the situation of a father who refuses to intervene in order to save his son from prison. But Martin too often sounds either like Ronnie or like the generalized voice of the younger generation, while Boomy sounds either like a little man given lofty lines ("My quarrel is with God not man") or like the stereotype parents ("I can't be expected to get excited about students' liberties").

The main trouble with the raw material Wesker chooses in *The Old Ones* is that it is very difficult to shape. The climax of Act One is provided by Boomy's narrative about how, at the age of sixteen, Emanuel threw a bag of diamonds into the Thames so that they could both live by the work of their hands. And in Act Two the montage which leads up to the revelation that Emanuel is speaking his own words, does not in any way prepare for it.

The final scene is the longest in the play. It begins as Rosa is telling the others how she eventually succeeded with her class of prospective graduates; it then goes into the religious ritual, which they abandon; this is followed by a philosophical argument between the two brothers about existence:

> EMANUEL: You idiot, you. The fact that you doubt is proof that you exist because you exist to doubt it.

A casual chat about children produces the revelation that Martin is in prison; a monologue from Rudi tells us how Martin, eager to see the inside of a nut-cracking factory, bribed half a dozen schoolchildren to play truant and pretend he was their teacher, so that he could take them around it; Emanuel and Gerda argue about cremation; Boomy has a long, badly placed speech about the violence of the *Lumpenproletariat*; Jack trots out a hobby-horse about an organ that could play smell-music by puffing out odors; Teressa tells a story about a Jewish woman who claimed conjugal rights from a sixty-five-year-old Danish poet who married her to save her from the Gestapo; Rosa proposes a toast to her mother, and they perform a Hasidic dance while the others hum and clap; Emanuel, who has been having a bath, bursts in, naked except for a towel, to announce a new and nonsensical definition of cruelty.

While actions lead into each other quite well enough, the thematic discontinuity of the conversation makes it impossible for Wesker to build up a final, driving momentum with it. Of course, the aimlessness of the people and noncommunication between them are essential points, but points it would have been hard to make theatrically. The basic theme and situation of *The Old Ones* are inimical to the kind of movement that the play form demands. As in *The Friends*, there is no dramatic dynamic. The play consists of little more than one long exposition.

The Journalists

The Journalists is the best play Wesker has written since *Chips with Everything*, and in it the cutting from one locale to another is still more filmic than in *The Old Ones*. Each of the four acts has over thirty scenes, some of them very brief, and there are a hundred and fifty-three scenes in all. The stage represents the various offices of a national Sunday newspaper of the caliber of the *Sunday Times*. The space, which needs to be divided into two or three levels, has to represent a large newsroom and eight other offices within the newspaper building: the editor's office, the foreign department, the business news section, arts and entertainment, the women's page, features and political news, sports, and "In Depth." There also needs to be a space for the scenes set outside the newspaper building. In all there are thirty-three characters, plus a miscellany of messengers, subeditors and reporters.

The life that revolves around a newspaper can simultaneously be treated naturalistically and used as a microcosm of a country's mental life. Wesker makes his editor define journalism as "an act of creating self-awareness in society," and in dramatizing the functioning of an important newspaper he shows quite a lot about how information is sifted and angled before it is printed. One of the columnists defines a journalist as "a man who possesses himself of a fantasy and lures truth towards it." Two others agree that a warning ought to be printed on the front page of every newspaper, saying: "The selective attention to data herein contained may warp your view of the world."

Wesker researched the play very thoroughly, spending two months sitting in at the offices of the *Sunday Times*, and he successfully reproduces the flavor of newspaper office conversations. The documentary element in the play can be seen as emerging out of his use of the tape recorder while writing *The Old Ones*, but it is given greater resonance in *The Journalists*. This is partly because of the play's wider perspective on recent world events.

Facts come pouring through the telex machines about the murder of two hundred and fifty Bangladesh intellectuals, and about the equally horrifying reprisals of the Mukti Bahani guerrillas. An American freelance reporter calls in claiming to have a trunkload of documents that reveal the truth about Biafra. An assistant sports editor boggles at the irony of going to Northern Ireland to cover a game of golf while soldiers and civilians are being killed. But the statement the play makes about newspapers and about self-awareness in society will go on being valid long after the events selected are no longer topical.

Important national issues are presented side-by-side with international ones. Mary Mortimer, the paper's star interviewer, is seen in action at the beginning of each act, putting questions to cabinet ministers. She confronts the Minister for Social Services with the fact that the quality of a democracy depends on the quality of the petty officials who administer it. She cross-examines the Minister for Science and Technology about the profit motive, challenges the Chancellor of the Exchequer over the disparity between his standard of living and that of the workers, and she gets drunk with the

Minister of State for Foreign Affairs. The editor ventilates the problem of why the nation's best brains do not go into politics. The Conservative government is pilloried in an argument over strategy and philosophy. There are also many references to current social, economic and political issues.

By switching very quickly from one room to another, by selecting from the conversations going on while material is being prepared for the next issue of the paper, Wesker is able to embrace a huge and and heterogeneous collection of themes, without developing most of them in terms of plot. But the trade union issue is very neatly knitted into the plot. Union action stops the messengers from working, and for a while it seems that the paper will not come out. In addition, a conflict develops between Mac Smith, an official of the union, and Ronnie Shapiro, the Jewish sports editor, who is father of the union's newspaper local.

A strike is threatened over a garage which is going to be closed, causing thirty men to be laid off. The employers have agreed to postpone the closure, but they have sent the staff a note saying that the union was asking for the decision about closing the garage to be withdrawn. The union now complains that its position has been misrepresented: all it asked was that the date announced for closure be withdrawn. A quibble which seems to involve a matter of principle can easily lead to wasteful and prolonged industrial warfare, but Ronnie gets the men back to work by promising Mac Smith that unless agreement is reached about the layoffs, he will persuade his local to give two weeks notice of strike. As he says after Mac has gone:

> We're clogged by irrelevant but all too vivid memories. Do you think that when a union leader sits facing an employer he's merely confronting a man who wants to pay him less than he's asking? Never! He's confronting a personality to whom he needs to show how he too can argue, be firm, touch, wield power. Have you ever seen

the conference rooms in trade union offices. Replicas of city board rooms.

This is not the main plot. A play like this, with so many disparate elements in it, needs a very strong story line. The latter is provided by a conflict between Mary Mortimer and a member of parliament whom we never meet, Morgan King. The editor describes him as "the new fiery socialist superstar." Many of the ideas Morgan King stands for are close to those Wesker has championed in earlier plays and in public campaigning. Opening the town hall in one of the new towns, Morgan King attacks "the dead spirit of the place," rather in the manner of *Their Very Own and Golden City*:

> There's no variety in the shapes we have here. Where are your wide roads and your rambling alleys, where are your bold squares and intimate corners? Where is your colour, your sound, your movement of line?

Like Wesker himself, Morgan King wants the public to see him as a whole man, "imperfections and all." Again like Wesker—or at least like the earlier Wesker—he believes in the possibility of redeeming the working classes by bringing culture to them:

> Clear away the undergrowth of ignorance and the rubble of fear, then you'll see all the patterns men can make for the pleasure of their living.

He also argues that pensioners should receive no less than the national minimum wage. Wesker does very well not to let Morgan King appear in the play. The nonappearance of Ronnie in *Roots* made the play much better than either of the others in the trilogy, and Morgan King's views, similarly, are more theatrically palatable when presented indirectly, filtered through the other characters.

Wesker shows a similar restraint in handling the plot's main climax. This hinges on a secret society. Harry, a news reporter, has uncovered a connection between an unofficial strike in South Wales, two kidnappings—one of a manager, one of a boss—a bank robbery, and cash payments to the strikers made anonymously through the mail. His investigations reveal that the society genuinely exists, and Mary Mortimer is meanwhile given information which convinces her that Morgan King was involved in it. Given an excellent opportunity to bring him down, she is determined not to miss it. But the editor finds out from Harry that one of her children is active in the society and, in a theatrical climax, he sends the final edition of the paper to press without the story he had promised to wait for. And nothing that Mary can say will make him explain.

One of the weaknesses of the play is that, as in *The Old Ones*, the characters tend to explain themselves rather than reveal themselves; but this matters less because there are so many more of them and because the sequences are so much briefer. The scale of the play is ambitious, and Wesker shows both confidence and skill in handling such a mass of material and so many characters unlike those types with which he is most familiar. Not all of his journalists are equally convincing —the women on the women's page and the men on the arts page come off the worst—but much of the dialogue has a crispness and an astringency which are new for Wesker. Some of it may not be above the level of average television drama, but arguably it constitutes an advance that so little of it is recognizable as having been written by him.

ANTHONY: You rang?

HARVEY: Tony, yes. I want you to do something on women being allowed into the stock exchange.

ANTHONY: Love to. Can't claim the privileges of a private club now, can they?

HARVEY: I was thinking of a light hearted leader, not an occasion for solemnity.

ANTHONY: Indeed not, no, indeed. They've made fools

enough of themselves. Now let's see if they're still
worried about telling dirty jokes on the floor. How
many words?
HARVEY: About 450?
ANTHONY: Done.

This is almost too anonymous, but the contrast with *Four
Seasons* could hardly be greater.

Wesker has also extended his range in characterization.
With most of the journalists he makes no attempt to penetrate
deeply into their guilts and sufferings. Where he does try
this, as with Tamara Drazin, the Jewish foreign correspon-
dent, he falls into the same boggy self-explication that spoiled
The Friends and damaged *The Old Ones*. But Mary and the
editor, Harvey, are both characterized by being shown in different situations, richocheting off a variety of people, reacting
to a variety of pressures. Ronnie Shapiro, though Jewish, is
refreshingly different from any of Wesker's earlier characters,
and the cabinet ministers whom Mary interviews, although
they have only one scene each, are written with more insight
and sympathy than the equivalent characters in *Their Very
Own and Golden City*. There is a lively vignette of a greedily
womanizing Irish journalist in the business news department,
and Mary's children are much more convincing than the rebel-
lious youngster in *The Old Ones*.

The Journalists is both one of Wesker's most disciplined
plays and one of his most relaxed. Certain points may be
underlined too heavily; for example, towards the end we get
too many repetitions of the point about the danger inherent
in a newspaper's selective attention to detail. But there is a
good deal of compensating comedy and vitality.

The organic movement of the play grows up around the
newspaper's movement towards the moment when, at about
six o'clock on Saturday evening, the printing presses start to
roll. Toward the end of the week, there is an inevitable
frenzy of last-minute activity as decisions are made about the

allocation of front-page space. The physical bustle may be very different from that of cooks and waitresses in a busy restaurant, but more than in any other play since *The Kitchen*, Wesker cashes in on the theatrical possibilities of large-scale corporate activity reaching a climax of intensity; and he shows the same talent for dramatizing it.

Halfway through the final act he calls for a film projection of the turning presses, and as they start we hear the full blast of their noise. The volume of this has to be taken down for the dialogue which is to follow, but the hurried movements of the messengers, the speed with which decisions have to be taken, the changing rhythm of the characters' speech patterns, and the rhythm of the sequence of short scenes all contribute to the climacteric accelerando. As in *The Kitchen*, the full potential of the play can be realized only with the help of a director capable of disciplining his actors into an intricate choreography of physical actions; but *The Journalists* is much more complex than *The Kitchen*, more carefully structured, with a more calculated interdependence of dialogue and movement.

Since the over-ambitious *Their Very Old and Golden City*, each of Wesker's plays had been less ambitious than its predecessor, but with no compensating consolidation of technical *savoir faire*. Now, suddenly, he has bounded ahead to write an extremely ambitious play in which his technique matches up to the demands he makes on it.

SECOND INTERVIEW*

Arnold Wesker: Let's start with your responses to the games in the plays. It seems to me that you dismiss with some embarrassment the game with the child in *Jerusalem*. Well it may be that if you were to have known me over a longer period of time and more intimately, you'd be embarrassed by me. Because these are games which we are quite capable of playing. The umbrella scene actually happened—it isn't something that I invented. When you don't respond to something like Sarah's lifting of the umbrella, which for me is a marvelous lunacy, then you miss a number of things. You say it's a private joke, well it is a private joke but it is not an obscure one. I think it's funny in its own right. It's a comment on Sarah's personality—I think it increases an awareness of the texture of this family's relationship. I think it is also a dramatic moment in the tense up-and-down in the ending of that scene, and it's something that works visually.

You quote a passage from *The Four Seasons* on page 100 which you find embarrassing, where Beatrice says "I have a golden eagle for a lover" and you say there is more bad writing in this play than in any other of Wesker's, but I would put it to you that it depends on how you read it because in fact those are words which lovers say to each other and I think that lovers, when they do say them, say

---

* What follows is an edited transcript of a taped discussion which went on for four hours.

them with a slight edge. Now I could have given a stage direction which would have gone something like this: "The next passage is to be tentatively delivered, each of them betraying a self-consciousness of their love words by giving a slightly self-mocking tone, watching each other to see how far they dare go both in their demands and their use of language." With such a stage direction, you'd have read the "I have a golden eagle" passage quite differently. And the way in which they use those very delicate words is parallel with the tentative way in which they make demands on each other. She's for instance not quite sure how far she can go, until finally, when he says "I deny you nothing"; then she gives a really great burst and says, "I have a golden eagle for a lover." And says that without shame. But all the rest—the love words and the content of the love words—is tentative. Another thing that you forget, it seems to me, is that they are out in the open. And one imagines them on the edge of a cliff shouting out to the gods "I have a golden eagle for a lover"—a very difficult thing for an actress to do. Diane Cilento was acutely embarrassed. The actress in Paris—and there the production was a great success—evaded it by saying it quickly and softly.

I think this may have a great deal to do with people's actual incapacity to know how to love fully . . . in these very inhibited times . . . they're tight . . . they haven't the ability to really burst out.

I wonder if there's a basic difference between us over whether we consider discussion to be dramatic or not. Now I happen to think that people caught up in an actual argument about ideas can be essentially dramatic as opposed to something theatrical and people scoring points on each other intellectually, or even opening out their hearts—being impassioned. This is for me drama. That scene in Chicken Soup, for instance, where they're sitting round a table and Ada says what I can see could appear to be Wesker putting out his ideas into a character, where she's talking about Dave being disillusioned and so on. That kind of conversation round the table actually took place in our house. People did speak like this. Sarah's last speech in *Chicken Soup* is more or less verbatim something that my mother said to me. Corporal Hill's opening passage in *Chips with Everything* comes straight from a letter that I wrote to someone in London immediately after our corporal had spoken to us like that on that day. Now this is dramatic to me.

RONALD HAYMAN: *What is dramatic in everyday life isn't necessarily what is dramatic in a theater. What makes a profound impression in a conversation may not work—I keep using the word* work *because this is the basis of all the judgments I've made: what works, to me, in a theater. But what you say to justify the games—that these actually happened in your life—is surely no more of a reason for including them than including anything else that happened in your life, like the conversation that we're having now, which would be dreadfully boring if it were enacted on a stage, obviously. Everything depends on the selection. I don't think that the fact that Corporal Hill's speech comes straight from what the man said is in any way a criticism against it—on the contrary, you've selected there something which works theatrically very well and in the right place in the play.*

But you're not saying about the game for instance at the end of *Jerusalem* "Here is a possible family scene or situation or event which I can see could in real life be fun or touching or revealing, but it is not the kind of real life event which actually transcribes on to the stage." You're not saying this, you're saying that the concept of such a game in itself is weak or embarrassing.

I'm quite willing to say now that I accept it totally as something that could happen in real life exactly in the way it happens on the stage.

Would you go on to say you could see it being transferred into dramatic terms but you don't think I have made that work?

I don't see how you could transcribe any of these games directly any more than Osborne has succeeded in transcribing the squirrels and bears game, or than you have, to my mind, in this conversation about the golden eagle in The Four Seasons. *I can accept that as something that lovers could say but not as dialogue. As a little boy I was always terribly fascinated in railway carriages by what lovers were saying to each other in the corner, whispering. This looks very dramatic if you don't hear what they're saying, but if you could actually transcribe the dialogue, it would probably be dreadfully dreary, and so many conversations which are marvelous when you're having them in bed with someone else, would be embarrassing in a play in the way that this is. I think it's only by really great poetry that this can be made acceptable in a theater. Otherwise you're forced into the kind of approach that Chekhov adopted, which is implying the direct emotion, rather than stating it.*

I'm not sure that if we went through Chekhov we wouldn't find similar explicit declarations.

But they'd be counterpointed more immediately by something else.

Well you see I think that the counterpoint should be taken for granted. The play should be acted *against*. You must work against the words. When you quote passages from *The Four Seasons* and say that they are mannered and self-intoxicated, I don't feel that they are mannered and self-intoxicated, though I am embarrassed by some passages you've quoted from the earlier plays. And then you take the last section of *The Four Seasons* and applaud that and I can't see what there is in the one passage that merits your approval and what there is in the other passage that merits your disapproval.

Really it's a matter of your being specific. In the passage I've quoted on page 101 the images and the phrases evoke particular memories and marshall them in a way that enables the audience to participate in the emotion without any danger of embarrassment.

You're not worried by words like "astonishment" and "burn" or "the tremendous blaze of dying hedges"?

They could be made to work by a good actress. In playing it she could be delving into her mind in a way that would be theatrical. In writing these phrases you've linked them together in a way which could help her to play the fact that something dramatic—by which I mean her trying to remember—is going on. The rhythm of the effort of memory is reflected in the rhythm of the language you've written for her.

But it seems to me that I'm doing the same things on page 95.

In writing dialogue you are evoking two pictures. I mean in reading it you've got to picture the actor on a stage and (in these two instances at least) you've also got to picture what the actor is picturing. In the passage on page 101 the language you've written produces pictures for me; here the phrases remain as phrases. It's really a matter of the relationship between one phrase and another. In that passage, each phrase arises out of its predecessor; one picture therefore emerges out of the previous one. Here [on page 95], first of all, he's talking about his wife in a way that doesn't produce a picture, then you get a phrase about another country which seems evasive of naming the country that he came from. "Eyes like an uncertain child" does in itself produce an image but "festive room" seems slightly artificial. And then the "deep pleasure," without exactly contradicting the uncertainty, doesn't seem to have the right relation to it. I think you need to tell me in your development of the images how he gains confidence. In the passage on page 101 the language seems absolutely right for the girl who is remembering. Here [on page 95] the language doesn't help Adam to voice his attitude. There seems to be a gap between the emotion he's feeling in remembering it and the emotion that these words and rhythms would evoke. "All the secret corners of our own past she revealed" is just a cliché, isn't it? But it isn't so much that as the structure of the prose. It's the way the points interrelate and build or fail to build, and whereas the other passage builds, this doesn't for me imply either the right kind of recollection going on in Adam's mind or the right kind of development in the relationship between his wife and the young man. I can't see it—it isn't unfolding for me in the way it should be from what you've written. It's a question of solidity.

On page 21 you say, "They are saying it in fact because he wants it to be said. He's using characters and situations to make points that were preoccupying him long before they were." I would like examples, because I think the points and the characters from out of the melee and noise in one's mind process of re-creating experiences is partly one of extracting the characters from out of the melee and noise in one's mind and attaching the right voices to the characters, the right tones that is, and sometimes in a second version one takes a speech from one character and gives it to another because it belongs to him. One has made a mistake in the assembly, in the stitching. I've cut the right shape from the cloth, but put the left arm on to the hole of the right arm. The voices have gotten mixed up, but they come at the same time.

One instance that occurs both in The Kitchen *and in* Jerusalem *is the preoccupation with working in factories as opposed to working as a craftsman works, individually. The preoccupation seems to come through in what the characters say, rather than to be arrived at together with the characters.*

Somewhere else I once said that the plays are extensions of discussions and quarrels I've had with friends and family and work colleagues, so that I've had things that some of the characters have said—they may not have been those actual characters, but they come from similar characters—perhaps when I was in the building trade, as a carpenter's mate, or with the chef in the kitchen in Norfolk, which is roughly two or three years before the kitchen in Paris; but the point is that ideas like these were all being talked about at the same time as I met the characters.

To me Dave's apprentice in Jerusalem *doesn't seem to get very individualized because he is used rather as a pawn in this argument with Dave.*

Then that's not inherent in the nature of what I'm writing—it's the failure of me to make it work. Because again, that's precisely what happened. That boy did have that relationship with my brother-in-law and finally left. Because he wanted more money. And that kind of discussion took place.

But isn't it a question of whether you're focusing on bringing the discussion to life or bringing to life the people who have the discussion?

Because I know that you can't do one without the other, I would like to think that I was trying to make them both happen. If the discussion has come out at the expense of the characters, then I haven't done what I wanted to do but I want it acknowledged that what I was trying to do was right, that there's a dramatic possibility in such a confrontation. But I don't think that's what you're reacting against. It's very difficult to avoid it, especially in England, where there's a detestation of the pronouncement of ideas. An Englishman doesn't like to be imposed on. And so it irritates us when we see two characters actually talking like this. That's why the English don't like the French.

I think there are passages in Golden City *where people are arguing and throwing ideas at each other where this is absolutely dramatic, but an example of what I'm objecting to is the tremendous speech at the end of* Roots, *which works theatrically extremely well; but after starting off from a concern with what Beatie is feeling at that moment, you become involved in an argument which was preoccupying you before—the whole question of culture. I'm not convinced that at that moment she would talk in that way about the working classes and their roots.*

It's possible to have people say anything at any odd moment, even though it seems impossible, providing the quality of the language is such that it raises the moment above its credibility.

You mean it's naturalistically wrong, but you're departing from naturalism here?

Yes. And you can do, even though the rest of the play has been naturalistic, because it's real in an oblique way. It's not a falsification of the truth, nor is it a testing of our credulity beyond what it can take. If you accept that, then you can only criticize the ending of *Roots* on the grounds that the order of writing is not big enough to detract from the unnaturalness that there is in her saying what she is saying at that particular moment.

But you can say that the rest of the play hasn't established a convention in which this sort of departure from naturalism is made acceptable.

How many times are there moments in our experiences of other people that we haven't been prepared for? So what? So it is out of character. It may be that something has happened that we didn't think was possible.

What I'm really worried about is that instead of documenting the Bryant kind of life better, you're giving the impression—which must be a false one—that they spend the bulk of their time arguing about culture. With Shaw I have the feeling that he is using his characters and his situations to make points. With you I sometimes get some of that feeling.

Well yes I am doing this. What I deny is that I'm making them say points out of character, that I'm grafting points on to the character.

I think the important question is whether an actress of Joan Plowright's caliber could play it as movingly and effectively today as she could in 1959. Because then in a way it gladdened all our hearts to hear those words being said so forcefully as such a key moment. It didn't in 1966—that may have been the actress's fault, although she's quite a good actress. Or it may be that there's something about the play which had a relevance then and hasn't now.

A la guerre comme à la guerre. . . . On page 34 you say that only an actor with great personal charm could save Ronnie from seeming tiresome. When you're saying Ronnie is tiresome in this passage you're also saying that I'm tiresome. Again that's a re-creation of a dialogue that I had with my mother. Perhaps I have great personal charm and it wouldn't have seemed tiresome if you'd witnessed it. . . . On page 36 you attack the language again as facile and rhetorical.

It sounds to me flat. It could come straight off the top of the character's head. I think this is a point where it isn't enough to reproduce the kind of language you might actually have used in an argument with your mother. What we need here is something sharper, something that forces the actor to go deeper into himself than that. What you haven't done is realize in words the force with which he's asking himself the question. He's deeply perplexed about whether the promises that were made to him and that he made to himself all along were justifiable at the time or whether for twenty years he has been deluding himself. It's a profound question which needs profound language.

In the midst of a family quarrel do you think that a character could reach out for profound language? Wouldn't he reach out for the simplest language?

The point is you've got to make it work theatrically. Often in our most moved moments we say a lot that would be very unimpressive on a stage. This does need to affect and involve the audience who are not in the same situation as he is. You have to communicate an emotion, which these words don't help the actor to do.

Now you seem to be confused by the flash-forwards in *Golden City*. What I'm trying to do with the flash-forward is keep us in a present in which there is still hope. I suppose I would view these first five or six or seven—I don't know quite how many—thousands of years it is—in the history of man as still being a present in which there's hope. In other words he hasn't completely canceled himself out. He still seems to have the energy to start again.

But I think there's a very uncomfortable division between two present tenses for the audience in the fact that the characters are situated in 1926 and we are situated in 1966 or whenever it is that we're watching it.

But the alternative would have been to have started in 1966 and to have written a futuristic play.

But as it is the future is divided into two slices—up to the point we have experience of and beyond it. You are writing about 1990 in the same kind of flash-forward as you're writing about 1966.

I don't know how to overcome this. This may be a failure but we're only in 1990 in the play because that happens to be the length of time it sensibly takes to do what they were trying to do. It wasn't an attempt to look into the future. I don't think I could have started in quite the same way in 1910, for instance.

I suppose the major drawback is the one I pointed out—that we aren't certain whether you regard the flash-forwards as fantasy or reality.

We can't be uncertain about that. The flash-forwards are not fantasy. We recognize them, don't we?

We recognize them up to the year we're in but not beyond.

I don't know why, because there's nothing that's happening that contains any element of fantastic futuristic——

The foundation of one Golden City—I never become convinced from the evidence you give us of the characters and their actions that even one Golden City could become a reality—it never does, for me, become a reality.

But we have Brazilia, don't we? We have the new towns.

Yes but they're not cooperative in the way the Golden Cities are.

It doesn't require a great stretch of the imagination—it's all possible.

But the play doesn't substantiate this. We don't know enough about what the Golden City is like.

Because that really isn't what it's concerned with. You say you can't visualize it. In one of the drafts I was going to have projections of the plans so that we could have visualized it, because I felt, as you do now, that unless one actually has a feeling for the City, one can't get excited about whether they fail or not. But it's not a play about the rights and wrongs of a particular shape in a city. However there is a passage in which I do attempt to indicate nevertheless what I think is architecturally an interesting city. It's where they say "What kind of city will it be?" in Scene Twelve.

But this is a scene set in 1926. This is what they're imagining, what they're planning. Surely one of the things that you absolutely must answer is how does this compare with the reality that they achieve. This is one of many hares you set loose that you don't even try to catch.

No, because at one point one of the characters says "The city is beautiful." In other words, architecturally it's all right.

But dramatically is that enough?

It isn't what the play is about so it seems to me enough to acknowledge that architecturally it works. But what the play is about is the spirit of the City, the relationships people have with each other which I see through the relationships people have with their work. Whether they're owning it or not. You know, the spirit of cooperation. This has failed and that's what's important, and I spend much more time lamenting that than having them pat themselves on the back because they've built a beautiful city.

But we never even hear what happens about the Monday meetings—when they stop. There are so many plans that are left in midair. What we need to know is the relationship between the reality they achieve—even in this context of flash-forward—and the original plan.

I think the play establishes a canvas within which so much is covered that it is possible to lose certain details.

You've said nothing about Chips.

I suppose I found *Chips* so easy to write that I can't believe it. I don't know why I don't like *Chips* so much. It came too naturally. You don't feel any effort, any struggle to carve anything out.

But in the theater we really do not want to know about what effort the playwright has experienced in writing the play.

I think we want to be able to feel that here is a man carving some shape out of his experience.

STAGE PRODUCTIONS

JULY 1958   *Chicken Soup with Barley,* directed by John Dexter, with Charmian Eyre and Frank Finlay, at the Belgrade Theatre, Coventry, and then at the Royal Court Theatre, London.

MAY 1959   *Roots,* directed by John Dexter, with Joan Plowright and Gwen Nelson, at the Belgrade Theatre, Coventry, and then at the Royal Court Theatre, London.

SEPTEMBER 1959   *The Kitchen,* Directed by John Dexter, with Robert Stephens, at the Royal Court Theatre, London.

MARCH 1960   *I'm Talking about Jerusalem,* directed by John Dexter, with Alan Howard and Cherry Morris, at the Belgrade Theatre, Coventry.

JUNE–JULY 1960   *The Wesker Trilogy,* all three plays at the Royal Court.

MARCH 1961   *Roots,* directed by Mark Rydell, with Mary Doyle and Katherine Squire, at the Mayfair Theatre, New York.

APRIL 1962   *Chips with Everything,* directed by John Dexter, with John Kelland and

	Frank Finlay, at the Royal Court Theatre, London.
OCTOBER 1963	*Menace*, directed by Herbert Wise, with John Hurt and Joanna Dunham, on BBC Television.
MAY 1966	*Their Very Own and Golden City*, directed by Bill Gaskill, with Ian McKellen and Ann Firbank, at the Royal Court Theatre, London.
JUNE 1966	*The Kitchen*, directed by Jack Gelber, with Rip Torn and Sylvia Miles, at the 81st Street Theatre, New York.
MARCH 1968	*The Four Seasons*, directed by Arthur A. Seidelman, with Paul Roebling and Barbara Hayes, at Theatre Four, New York.
DECEMBER 1969	*The Friends*, directed by Arnold Wesker, Statstheater, Stockholm.
MAY 1970	*The Friends*, directed by Arnold Wesker, with Ian Holm and Victor Henry, at the Roundhouse, London.
AUGUST 1972	*The Old Ones*, directed by John Dexter, with Max Wall and George Pravda, at the Royal Court Theatre, London.
1973	*The Journalists* is scheduled for production by the Royal Shakespeare Company during the 1973 season.

BIBLIOGRAPHY

PLAYS

Chips with Everything. London: Jonathan Cape, 1962; New York: Random House, 1962.

The Four Seasons. London: Jonathan Cape, 1968.

The Friends. London: Jonathan Cape, 1972.

The Kitchen. London: Penguin Books, 1960; New York: Random House, 1961.

Their Very Own and Golden City. London: Jonathan Cape, 1966.

The Wesker Trilogy. London: Jonathan Cape, 1960; New York: Random House, 1961.

   Chicken Soup with Barley. London: Penguin Books, 1959.

   Roots. London: Penguin Books, 1959.

   I'm Talking about Jerusalem. London: Penguin Books, 1960.

TELEVISION PLAY

Menace. The Jewish Quarterly, Spring 1963.

BOOKS

Fears of Fragmentation. London: Jonathan Cape, 1970.

Journey into Journalism. London: Jonathan Cape, 1972.

Six Sundays in January. London: Jonathan Cape, 1971.

SHORT STORIES

"The Hill." *The Jewish Quarterly*, Autumn 1958.
"Pools." *The Jewish Quarterly*, Winter 1958–59.

ARTICLES

"Let Battle Commence." *Encore*, November–December 1958.
"To React—To Respond." *Encore*, March–April 1959.
"Art Is Not Enough." *Twentieth Century*, February 1961.
"The Secret Reins." *The Observer*, 7 July 1963.
"The House." *Encounter*, November 1966.
"Delusions of Floral Grandeur." *Envoy*, October 1967.
"Casual Condemnations—A Study of the Critic as Censor." *Theatre Quarterly*, April 1971.
"From a Writer's Notebook." *Theatre Quarterly*, May 1972.

SELECTED CRITICISM ON WESKER

Amis, Kingsley, "Not Talking About Jerusalem," *The Spectator*, 10 August 1962.

Brustein, Robert, "Fragment from a Cultural Explosion," *The New Republic*, 27 March 1961.

Clurman, Harold, "Theatre," *The Nation*, 26 October 1963.

Hatch, Robert, "Arise, Ye Playgoers of the World," *Horizon*, July 1961.

Jones, A.R., "The Theatre of Arnold Wesker," *The Critical Quarterly*, Winter 1960.

Leech, Clifford, "Two Romantics: Arnold Wesker and Harold Pinter," in *Contemporary Theatre*, New York: St. Martins Press, 1962.

Leeming, Glenda, and Trussler, Simon, *The Plays of Arnold Wesker*, London: Gollancz, 1971.

Ribalow, Harold V., *Arnold Wesker*, New York: Twayne, 1965.

Taylor, John Russell, *The Angry Theatre*, New York: Hill and Wang, 1962.

INDEX

141